REINCARNATION

© DANIEL P. CURTIN

ABOUT THE AUTHOR

Marilou Trask-Curtin is the author of *Dreaming of the Dead: Personal Stories of Comfort and Hope* (Llewellyn, 2012) and *In My Grandfather's House: A Catskill Journal* (ProStar Publications, 2006). She is also a playwright, screenwriter, and songwriter. Trask-Curtin has had articles published in *Good Old Days*, *Ideals*, and *FATE Magazine*. She has been interviewed on *The X-Zone* as well as several local radio and television shows. The author lives with her husband in her childhood home in upstate New York, where many of her spirit encounters occurred and still occur today.

Please visit her website at www.mariloutrask-curtin.com.

*One Woman's Exploration
of Her Past Lives*

REINCARNATION

MARILOU TRASK-CURTIN

Llewellyn Publications
Woodbury, Minnesota

FIRST EDITION
First Printing, 2014

Cover art: Cover photo of author at age four provided by Marilou Trask-Curtin
   WL003949/Slede Preis/PhotoDisc/Getty Images
   78373779/Brand X Pictures/Stockbyte/Getty Images
   23687164/Paul Grecaud/iStockphoto.com
Cover design by Ellen Lawson

Llewellyn Publications is a registered trademark of Llewellyn Worldwide Ltd.

Library of Congress Cataloging-in-Publication Data
Trask-Curtin, Marilou, 1951–
 Reincarnation : one woman's exploration of her past lives / Marilou Trask-Curtin. — First edition.
  pages cm
 ISBN 978-0-7387-3897-0
1. Trask-Curtin, Marilou, 1951– 2. Reincarnation—Biography. I. Title.
 BL520.T73A3 2014
 133.901'35—dc23
        2013043230

Llewellyn Publications
A Division of Llewellyn Worldwide Ltd.
2143 Wooddale Drive
Woodbury, MN 55125-2989
www.llewellyn.com

Printed in the United States of America

Dedication and Acknowledgments

To my dearly loved grandparents, Edward and Myrtle Mc-Nally, who believed in me and my dreams and never once discouraged me from discussing unpopular topics like ghosts. Their faith in me endures beyond eternity, and I am very grateful to have been their daughter of the heart.

To my husband, Dan, who listens patiently and believes.

To Butch: my heavenly angel, my guide, always there in spirit with encouragement, advice, and some great ideas. From Atlantis to eternity your love sustains me always. LUV you forever, babe.

To our sweet cat, Pretty, who as always spent lots of time purring at me as I was writing this book. Also to our much loved "garage" cat, Gentleman TJ Gold: thanks for showing up in our lives. We love you both so much!

To Amy Glaser and everyone at Llewellyn Worldwide: thank you for everything you do.

My deepest gratitude is offered to those who have mentored me in this lifetime and put me on the life path I was meant to follow.

To the souls I have met and re-met on my present life path, who have shared love and friendship with me in other times and places—I thank you for being with me again. To those who were my enemies and adversaries in another time and place and who have shown up in my present, I also thank you. You have taught me valuable lessons I will never forget about forgiveness, acceptance, and letting go. Go in peace, and may the lessons we learned erase the karmic debt that once attached us.

To all those who wonder at the incongruity of life—the so-called "chance" meetings and "random" events, both good and not so good: may this book be a beacon that dispels the darkness and allows a new way of thinking and believing to enter your hearts and minds.

Contents

FOREWORD

Have you ever felt as if you've visited a particular place before, even though it's your very first time there? Or perhaps you have felt attracted to, or repelled by, a particular time period—or even a particular person. And have you ever wondered why so many children seem to have extraordinary talents, such being able to play a musical instrument without ever having taken one lesson?

If the answer to any of the wonderings above is "yes," then you may be dealing with a life spent in another time and place. And that child with remarkable ability—he or she may be simply exhibiting a skill from another lifetime.

For some of us, details of past lives trickle in through our dreams when we are deeply asleep. Others utilize a technique or therapy, such as past-life regression. And some of us seem just to *know* that we have lived before, and this knowledge comes to us at a very young age. There are entire books and websites devoted to children who remember their past lives.

Young children, often as soon as they are able to speak and while still in diapers, will talk about their "other parents" or "other homes." Some are able to remember their names and the names of family members in those other lives. Many recall exactly how they died in either a recent or distant time period. These children recall their past lives often with such emotional maturity and vivid detail that they prove to researchers all over the world that this is a phenomenon worth looking into. These young children are so much more socially unconditioned than adults and will often speak of their other lives in a factual tone. They will preface such memories with "I remember when I died and/or lived before…" or "When I was a grown-up last time and had children, their names were…" Many times the information they give is verified by well-known professionals.

If we accept what these gifted children tell us, we can never look at them in the same light again. We can no longer view them as inferior to us simply because they are young. They are no longer tiny biological beings shaped by heredity and environment. They are souls encased in a physical body who have lived and loved, known joy and hardship, raised children of their own and then died, and their souls have returned to life in new bodies. They bring in wisdom to us collected from those other lifetimes, and they have so much to teach us if we will listen.

Over 60 percent of the people in the world believe in some form of reincarnation. It might be a natural assumption that it is only Buddhists and Hindus who believe, but would it surprise you to know that one out of every four Americans believes that souls do return again and again in different bodies? Reincarnation offers a system of justice and balance in a world that can otherwise seem at times random, cruel, or unfair. It offers an explanation as to why one child might be born into a happy, healthy home with loving parents, while another child is born into a destructive third-world country, orphaned, neglected, and fighting for her life.

One of the most well-known and respected collections of scientific data that provides undeniable evidence that reincarnation is real is the life's work of the late Dr. Ian Stevenson. For over forty years, Dr. Stevenson collected, documented, and published thousands of cases of children, mostly between the ages of two to five, who spontaneously remembered a past life. Dr. Stevenson would identify and verify the deceased person that a child remembered being. He would then verify all the facts of the deceased person's life. He also matched birthmarks and birth defects of the children to wounds, usually fatal, that had brought about death in the child's previous lifetime, and these would be verified by actual medical records.

Past-life regression therapy is based on the premise that we are eternal beings who carry forward experiences from one lifetime to another. From our soul level we choose each life. We choose our families, friends, and even our pets. We choose challenges and often difficult lessons to help bring us to a place of balance, unconditional love, and unity.

As a past-life regression therapist, I have worked with many adults who have vividly recalled their past lives. Many of their fears and challenges in this current life can be explained by a past-life experience. An intense fear of water may be a result of drowning in a past life. An overwhelming fear of heights may be traced back to a fatal fall. An addiction to food may be related to starving to death in another lifetime. An intense dislike toward a family member or co-worker may be related to something that person did to you in another time and place. On the positive side, the incredible feeling of falling in love at first sight is often an indication of a deep and everlasting union that has brought your soul and your beloved one back together again for yet another chance to grow and learn. The love of playing a particular musical instrument is also carried over from a past life, as are the love and abilities of dancing, singing, cooking, writing, teaching, healing, and so many more passions and gifts.

My friend Marilou Trask-Curtin was one of the remarkable children who vividly recalled her past lives from the time she was an infant. In this amazing book she writes beautifully of her journey back to remembering who she was/is and why her soul returned to earthly life. This story, told with such great insight, offers all of us a way to remember. I truly believe that Marilou's book will unlock new doors in our minds and souls, and for those with an open mind we will never look at our lives in the same way again.

I honor and congratulate Marilou for her courage and her artistry in writing this book, and I acknowledge you, the reader, to make no mistake—you were meant to read this.

Open your heart and mind, and allow Marilou's true and heartwarming story to enrich and transform your life.

Diana M. Kenyon
Past-Life Regression Therapist
Binghamton, New York
www.my-pastlife.com

This is what I know to be true:
We all have, for the most part, been taught wrongly.
We are not bodies with souls, but rather
We are souls with bodies that we utilize
To gain experiences on earth.
When we reincarnate, we are given a new body
For our soul to abide in while we continue to
Learn and grow in lifetime after lifetime.
—Marilou Trask-Curtin

Introduction

Being born once is a miracle.

Living, dying, and being born again and again into new earthly lives has, for me, been a continuation of the miracle.

That knowledge was not something I understood as a very young child, but it is something I felt on a very deep soul level.

As the word *reincarnation* was not a part of my vocabulary when I was an infant or even a young woman in my early thirties, I came to call this phenomenon of thought and feeling that I had been here on Earth before, as different people who lived in different times and places, a *knowing*.

As remarkable as it may sound, this knowing first began when I was an infant and manifested itself in a rather interesting and unexpected way when I was fully conscious of my present earth age as being just three months.

It is with great vividness and clarity that I recall the late summer day I woke up in my crib from my afternoon nap. I was lying on my back, and I turned my head to the right and saw the familiar dappled patterns of sunlight moving about on the shade that was pulled down in the bedroom I shared with my grandparents—the two who had been my parents since I was newborn.

I could hear no voices coming from anywhere in the house, and indeed everything seemed wrapped in a deep stillness and peace.

I decided to try again a sort of exercise I'd been doing my best to master for the past several days.

I lifted my left hand up and tried to focus my eyes on it and hold it steady. As soon as I did that, my hand seemed to take on a life of its own and began to move jerkily away from me and then toward me. The inability to master the coordination necessary to hold my hand steady made me angry, and the rising emotion seemed to cause my hand to move forward quickly and hit me on the forehead. Not wanting to give up, I tried again and again and got the same results. It was so very frustrating and discouraging to me that I could not gain control over this appendage—a control I suddenly realized and *knew* I'd had once before in some other time and place. Totally upset with myself, I let my hand fall back down and began a slow whimper that escalated into a whining cry.

Very soon I was rewarded by the sound of the bedroom door creaking all the way open and my dear grandmother coming into the room, pulling up the shade, and then picking me up and cradling me in her arms before she put me on her bed for a changing. Then it was out to the kitchen where a warm bottle of milk awaited me.

As I lay cuddled in Grandma's arms on the wooden chair behind the big, black kitchen woodstove, I played with the large safety pin Grandma always used to hold the towel on my glass bottle—the hand towel that prevented me from "getting burned," as she put it.

In the midst of my contentment of being loved and fed, my thoughts were spinning in a frenzied blend alternating between erratic and cohesive—as if something in my brain was desperately trying to fuse itself together at a very accelerated pace.

I looked up at Grandma's sweet face looking down at me and basked in the peace and absolute love that shone at me from her dear gaze. On another level, and for the first time, I sensed a deep, deep sadness in her countenance but could not determine what that all-encompassing remorse may have been caused by. It was to me more of a darkness that filled the space around her physical form, and I had the sensation that my presence was an incredibly comforting thing for her.

My thoughts continued their flurried momentum.

Suddenly, as if tapping into some ancient memory bank, I *knew* beyond knowing that I had once been able to speak and walk and write and run!

I had been somewhere else before I had been here in this body.

This flash of memory was like a brilliant starburst of light going on in my head, and I marveled at it.

I stopped sucking my bottle as this amazing feeling and the accompanying visions swept through my small form like a gigantic surge of electricity. Grandma, thinking I was done with my bottle, began to draw it away from my mouth. The milk bubbled in the nipple, alerting me to what she was doing, and I whimpered and she gave it back.

I drank slowly and remembered as a kaleidoscope of images collided in my mind's eye.

There had been other children and grown-ups with me in that long-ago time, and then I was alone. I was a boy standing in a sunlit courtyard. Another boy about my age as lithe as I was—a boy with velvety soft brown eyes—stood beside me. There was a tall man with piercing blue eyes talking to us, but I couldn't hear the words he was saying.

The scene shifted rapidly. Now I was a girl—tall, slim, and dark-haired, looking sadly out over a desert scene.

I had cognizance of the words I was thinking and what they meant. I knew that I was looking at images of me when I had been here before.

I also knew that I had returned here from someplace very special and that the someplace I had come from was both very near and also extremely far away. The place I had come from was *home*. The next word I heard in my mind was *left*.

Intense feelings of loss and disconnection swept through me.

I was far from home and I had been left here!

An overwhelming sensation of incredible helplessness and longing overtook me, and I felt as if I were being pushed and pummeled by a tidal wave of emotions.

I tried not to whimper as I lay in Grandma's arms, because I knew she would not understand.

There was nothing I could do with my newfound knowledge because I understood that I was, for the time being, hopelessly trapped in a physical form that would, I knew, keep me prisoner for a long time before I would be able to talk to anyone about what I was experiencing.

I also knew that, if I were patient, this heavier-than-air new Earth body I was recently encased in would one day be able to run, play, and communicate to others the wonders I had known in those other beautiful places I had once lived in—the most beautiful of all being my true *home*.

Yes, I wanted to scream out in frustration at the limitations being reborn had created, but I kept silent—drinking my milk and waiting impatiently for the day when this new earthly body could communicate with the world.

Time would pass quickly, and just a few years after this awakening I would have the first of three near-death experiences and find myself able to communicate with the spirits of deceased loved ones and pets—first in form and later in dreams. My extremely detailed and vivid memories of these times are chronicled in my book *Dreaming of the Dead: Personal Stories of Comfort and Hope*—a book that has thankfully brought a great deal of comfort to its readers.

It is my sincerest hope that this new book, *Reincarnation*, will reawaken your soul to the limitless possibilities of reincarnation and the healing power of believing.

Chapter One

BEFORE WE BEGIN

I truly believe that every spiritual journey we embark on begins with both a curiosity and a dissatisfaction with the old beliefs we have held so dear—the beliefs we have clung to since childhood—and that somehow no longer resonate with what we yearn to understand. One day, many of us simply wake up to the *possibilities* that there are so many other ideas, doctrines, theories, and beliefs that we should at least attempt to explore.

Indeed, we should open our minds and ask that most valid two-word question, "*What if?*"

What if death is not the ending but a glorious new beginning that offers solace to our weary souls and grants us a time of rest between lives?

What if our immortal souls do return to earthly life in new bodies, and this return gives us another chance for true love and also grants us an opportunity to make things right with those we have wronged in another time and place?

What if reincarnation is *real*?

It is, I know, never, ever easy to turn one's back on the traditional teachings of our youth. To have faith in other beliefs and traditions can almost seem like a betrayal to those who raised us.

I know, because I've been there.

There may be an almost shameful feeling attached to wanting to explore such topics. But if you are like me, there comes a time when the curiosity takes hold and you find yourself purchasing that first book or watching television shows on the theme that has caught your attention—ghosts, for example. And even though the new interest in the paranormal or past lives has taken hold, many can't or won't speak aloud to their family members, friends, neighbors, or workmates about their newfound topic or topics of interest.

The whole thing seems somehow "wrong" or too New Age—and yet the allure of wanting to know more grows and builds inside until one day a tentative question or two is asked. If you are lucky, the person you are speaking with has that open mind or shares an experience of their own with you, and you find that you are not alone. Others also have had the same wonderments, and you begin to feel a lot better about the new things you are learning.

I have met so many of these skeptical and hopeful yet timid people while out doing book signings and speeches on the subjects of my three near-death experiences and my heavenly communications with those who have passed to spirit. At nearly every one of my public events, there are the curious ones, and when I meet these people I am so grateful because they are just opening to new possibilities of thought about their own mortality or that of a loved one or pet.

At book signings I will get someone who stops by, picks up my book *Dreaming of the Dead*, reads the back cover, and then asks, "What's this about?" I calmly explain what I have gone through since I was age three. Most listen intently and then suddenly remember a relative telling of an experience with ghosts (but in whispered tones as these subjects were pretty much taboo until recently) or a strange dream they had themselves that featured a departed loved one. The doorway is opened and they usually buy the book, seemingly grateful that such a story has been written and they now feel comforted that others have had these experiences.

Later, after they have read my book, they will get in touch with me via email or on my website and relate just how much reading the book helped them and that they are now passing it on to a friend or relative who is grieving.

Still, again, I know it is not easy to let go of the old ways and find the courage to ask the questions and seek the answers to that amazing two-word question "What if?"—and so I offer here an introduction to what reincarnation means to me and the lessons I have learned along the way.

What Reincarnation Means to Me

On a deeply personal level I believe reincarnation offers not only me but all of us a chance—or many chances—to unburden our souls of the wrongs we have done to others during our previous lifetimes on Earth. It also offers joyful reunion in physical form and a chance to renew love denied or cut short by often tragic circumstances.

To me, reincarnation is so much more than the mechanics of the death of the physical body, a resting time for the soul in Heaven or elsewhere, and then that soul returning to earthly life in a new body. To my way of thinking, this train of thought is far too simple an explanation for what I know is the incredible and fantastic journey that a soul might take from earthly life to Heaven and back again to earthly life to inhabit that new physical form. From my own experiences with reincarnation, these returns to earthly life are done with such incredible timing, pinpoint perfection, and accuracy that it boggles the mind and brings to knowledge the fact that there is indeed some great deity or majestic force operating in the universe that causes this to happen. Some call it God or the universe.

It cannot be any other way.

Why?

Because if we are to be able to re-meet or reunite across perhaps centuries of time to settle or complete what lies between us and another soul, then we must come together at a defining moment. There must be some sort of alignment of age and precise timing so that the souls find themselves in a circumstance that allows the event that brought them together in the first place to have an opportunity to play out once more.

It would do no good, to my way of understanding, if we were to reunite with someone we needed to learn a life lesson with and that person was so incredibly young that there could be no chance at all to unburden our souls of a karmic debt incurred in another lifetime. And, when this type of thing does occur—which it sometimes does—I have no explanation I could offer for such a disparity in age and time unless there had been some sort of "glitch" or purposeful delay in the aligning of the souls returning together. Maybe one of the embodied souls was somehow allowed to live longer to complete a mission assigned by the universe, such as the finalization of a grand tour that would bring enlightenment to millions.

It seems at least plausible.

During my last near-death experience in 1984, when I was taken to Heaven by my guardian angel and saw my loved ones and pets that had passed to spirit, I was charged with a mission by my angel. Indeed, my angel told me we are all given missions to complete on Earth, and whether these missions are earth-changing ones or something not so dramatic but meaningful nonetheless, the angel admonished me that these missions must be completed before a return home to Heaven can be allowed.

This then resonates with not only a time lag that may be granted to some souls to complete their Earth missions but also, to my way of thinking, that these "missions" the angel spoke of are also about learning forgiveness, acceptance, love, compassion, sympathy, and empathy for one another. It might be as simple as learning to say "I'm sorry" and meaning it or as complex as being a force that helps to bring a mass of people to understanding and good.

Perhaps the powers of the universe grant a pardon to some that causes a ripple effect into the future lives of those souls waiting to reincarnate and complete what lies between them—whether it be joyful reunion or karmic debt.

But I truly believe that in love or even tormented relationships, the souls most often seem to return to fulfill what was unfulfilled in another lifetime. I know because as we shall see in later chapters, it has happened for me on several occasions.

And these seemingly random meetings, at least to me, were and are all about timing.

Again, I truly believe that timing is everything—both here on Earth and in the celestial realms. That means that precision is required to get the same souls back together so that they can reunite, continue their stories, or right the wrong between them and move ever closer to that glorious return *home*.

On a simplistic level and as an example, let's say that way back in the 1700s you fought with your neighbor because of a dispute over property lines. That act of cruelty causes a ripple effect through the centuries that blots your soul with a negative impact. It also causes a karmic bond or debt between you two that must be paid back so that your souls can move forward on their spiritual paths. It's the old "What goes around comes around" theory in operation.

In order for your soul to become unblemished, you and your neighbor must meet again in another time and place— same souls, different bodies and times. However, circumstances may be vastly different—or they could remain the same. Your neighbor may still be your neighbor, or he could even be a relative in your new lives.

However it works out, one day an event occurs that causes tempers to flare over something to do with property. At that precise moment, your soul has a choice—either resolve the problem with kindness and fairness, or revert to the old, cruel way of dealing with the issue. If you and your neighbor decide to fight again instead of working things out, more karmic debt is incurred and the story continues until you/your soul enters a lifetime where you have the wisdom to work things out and the karmic debt between you is erased.

The karmic debt will continue until the problem is somehow resolved in a peaceful and forgiving manner.

Reincarnation also gives lost lovers a chance to reunite across centuries—to complete the story, to share the kisses and the joy of being together once again even if it is for a small amount of time. It offers solace to those who had a loved one pass to spirit before the relationship came to fruition. It gives a sure way to resolve differences and lay the past to rest. It also offers up reasonable explanations for the diversity and frequent incongruity in human lives—health, wealth, fame, poverty, failure, joy, achievement, and so much more.

Reincarnation explains away the seeming randomness of events—both good and bad—that really are not random at all.

I know this is all true, because my life has proven it to be so.

KARMIC DEBT

If I take a loan out from a bank, it is expected that I will have to pay that loan back in full in order to return the balance to zero and eradicate the debt.

It's pretty much the same with karmic debt, except you are operating on a soul level.

As with my prior illustration of the neighbor you fought with in another time and place, karmic debt once incurred must be paid back—much like the bank loan. If the debt is not paid back, interest—in this case, more soul debt—accumulates. The punishment for nonpayment or continuing with negative behavior toward the wronged one prevents you from returning *home* for good and finally—unless you request a return to earthly life—getting off the wheel of death and rebirth, which to many is a most desirable event.

All souls yearn to go *home*. And I'm not talking about the earthly home of wood or stone or wherever else you lay your head down at night to sleep. No. This home is one of joy, peace, health, reunion, and total unconditional love. It may be called by many names: Heaven, Paradise, the Summerland, or Valhalla, but it is all the same place. It is the place I have been privileged to visit on three occasions after near-death experiences during my present earthly incarnation and the place no one wants to come back from.

So, is earthly life a punishment?

Perhaps some of it is.

Because for most of us, life here, whether it be our first incarnation or our thirty-first, is usually a blend of joy and sorrow, light and shadow. And I believe this is as it should be. How else are we to learn the lessons we need to advance forward on our journey to our true *home*?

Or, put another way—there must be shadows or we would not appreciate the beauty of the light.

Since I have undergone past-life regression, had my three near-death experiences, and been in communication with the dead in both form and dream visits from them, I have developed my own understanding of what being reborn means and what life here is about. To me, Earth is nothing more than a gigantic schoolhouse where all souls learn valuable lessons and make choices for good or not so good every single day—choices that impact not only our own souls, but the souls of others as well.

Choices that echo in eternity.

I'VE BEEN BOTH MALE AND FEMALE?

Well, now it gets interesting.

Yes, again from my own experience, I know that we souls reincarnate throughout the years or centuries and most often alternate between being males and females.

To me, from my very first past-life memory and later during my first regression session, this was a bit of a surprise, but—as I settled into the time period I found myself in and gave it a great deal of thought after the session was over—I realized that this switch from one gender to the other made perfect sense, because the male and female perspective on life and the world at large is often vastly different.

I feel that the female perspective views things from a more emotional standpoint while a male is more analytical and action-oriented—nothing scientific here, just my observations of the genders.

I see this switching between genders as an extremely well-balanced way for a soul to learn.

The experiences one has as a boy or man offer up lessons on acuity, perception, practicality, and, one hopes, making decisions based on strategy that will bring about a win-win situation for all involved. There must be a stepping away and getting the big picture before taking action. Rarely—and maybe sadly—many of the decisions made by men down through the ages have lacked a great deal of emotional involvement.

A woman's soul is based in heart and feeling and emotions. Yes, she can be as practical and as ruthless as a man during a crisis, but there will usually be deep understanding, compassion, sympathy, and empathy for others in whatever decision she is about to make.

The combination of having been able to walk this earth incarnated alternately as both male and female offers a blending of all the best (and sometimes the worst) of the human attributes.

We have all met women who are greedy, self-seeking, and power-hungry, and there seems not an ounce of compassion or kindness in them. We have also met men who are full of the gentle qualities of understanding and caring and that exhibit no ruthlessness toward their fellow humans.

For me, reincarnation offers the explanation to these behaviors.

Simply put, the ruthless and power-hungry woman with not an ounce of kindness visible perhaps enjoyed too much the power of being male in another time. The man who is kind and compassionate to a fault may be resonating to a previous lifetime as a woman who was all about love and empathy.

In the end result, I believe that the powers that be, those higher guides who reside in the celestial realm who gently but firmly lead us toward our destinies, seek for us to be a combination of all the best emotional attributes of both genders, and so we are given opportunities to learn by being both, to return as both male and female over several lifetimes.

In the end, every soul's ideal would be to manifest the balance of good in both genders in order to advance on their particular soul's journey to *home.*

I'VE COME BACK AS MY MOTHER'S SISTER?

Or your own grandfather or your father's brother—and the list goes on.

Reincarnation definitely happens in just this way and in many other combinations as well.

It is very nearly tribal and family- and community-oriented, and from what I understand these groups tend to reincarnate together. From my observations, family seems to be the best venue for working out karmic debt. In this lifetime, my mother and I have always felt that we were twin sisters in another time and often comment to one another that we feel more of a sisterly tie than a mother-daughter one.

As far as family ties go, take a moment if you can to read some of the cases that the late Dr. Ian Stevenson recorded with young children. There are literally thousands of documented studies this psychiatrist-turned-past-life-researcher did with young children. After Dr. Stevenson's death, one of his colleagues, Dr. Jim Tucker, carried on the work.

My favorite case is of the young boy named "Sam," who upon seeing never-before-looked-upon photos of his late grandfather, recognized his present-day self as the reincarnation of the elderly man. Sam also recognized his grandfather's car as his and picked his own/his grandfather's face out of a class picture.

Just amazing! And it validates my own *awakening* at age three months and the deep knowing I had by age three.

There are a myriad of ways that the universe teaches via reincarnation.

Perhaps a husband in another lifetime reincarnates as the wife the next time and the wife is now the husband, and so forth.

Again, when looked at from the perspective of the learning the soul must do, it makes perfect sense.

And this switching of roles and genders in family and relationships offers an incredible way for the soul to learn and progress or sometimes even backslide and learn even more on its journey *home*.

A prime example of this learning in relationships happens when a spouse or partner cheats on the other. Karmic debt is incurred by all parties involved due to the negative emotions of betrayal, disloyalty, loss of trust, and all the accompanying life upheavals. Seeking to create balance and pay off the karmic debt, this group will reincarnate in another time and place where they will be given choices that will pay off their debt or keep them on the wheel of rebirth.

Do I Know You From Somewhere?

There is no real tried and true method for recognizing someone you have known in a past life, but there are a few guideposts I have found that are pretty reliable.

First and foremost, for me at least, comes the *feeling* of connectedness at the moment of first meeting—especially if this is a reunion based on a positive past-life experience.

It is as if at that first contact, or upon seeing the person, you know intuitively that there is something incredibly familiar about them. When you get a chance to meet and talk together, it is as if you are old and dear friends reuniting and simply catching up on news of one another's lives. There is a continuity and a feeling of having spent a time apart, but everything is okay now because you are communicating and being in one another's presence again. And it feels so good to be there! It makes you feel complete on every level, and you walk away from that re-meeting with a soul peace that fills your heart.

Again, this event may seem to be random, but it is anything but. I have always felt that any re-meeting was/is timed down to the last second because it was somehow imperative that you reunite. This can happen at the most interesting of places: standing in a checkout line, after a fender-bender, in a group, at a park—seemingly anywhere people congregate. Lately, a lot of it happens online on dating sites.

Many of my more recent re-meeting experiences have occurred at book signings. I look up, and there standing or seated beside me is a person with a look about them that seems to shout, "Don't I know you?" Within minutes we have connected on a deep soul level and are talking about the most intimate details of our lives as if we already knew about them. Truly, some of this may be attributed to the types of books I write—those that deal with human emotions, love, family, and subjects that concern all of us like death and Heaven— but that only explains part of it.

The connections go way beyond that.

"I Don't Like You Very Much"

Just as there are reunions on a soul level that bring joy and love into our lives, there are also those relationships fraught with negative emotions. These are the people we meet who instantly put us off, or even repulse us. We find ourselves immediately distrusting the other, being unable to meet their eyes or to even be in their presence—and yet, on a purely unemotional level, there is no real reason for any of these feelings.

But the soul remembers them.

In contrast to the comforting re-meeting relationships that make us feel at ease and connected at the outset, these relationships where we feel on guard and uncomfortable also serve a purpose and, again, we must understand that we are brought together again with unerring precision.

These are the relationships that have the lessons attached and, indeed, when I find myself in one of these, I pay very close attention.

For me at least, one of the most peculiar things I have found is that most of these tough soul-lesson teachers usually arrived in my life in the form of family or workmates—and these teachers are usually women. I never understood this in my youth, just thinking there was something in my psyche that attracted girlfriends who were often just plain nasty to me for no apparent reason. Later, and after my regression to a particular lifetime, I began to understand what was happening and the thing became much clearer to me—in most cases I had a karmic debt to pay back, and it was usually earmarked with the tags of my learning forgiveness and acceptance, and coming to understand why that person had shown up in my life at that particular moment.

I recall one such difficult incident that later echoed with great clarity in my mind and for my soul's journey.

I had written a play, and that play was accepted by a theater and was in the process of being rehearsed. It was so very wonderful to actually see my characters come to life through the voices and emotions of some marvelous actors. I was flying high with joy and pride and disbelief that something that I had written would actually be performed on stage and be seen and enjoyed by my friends, relatives, and—I hoped—many others.

Fast forward about two weeks into rehearsal when one of the people in charge of the production pulled the rug out from under me. There were serious issues broached by this person that eventually brought me to the decision to pull the production.

I was very deeply hurt by this situation and by the betrayal I experienced, but I truly saw no other way out of the dilemma.

The actors who had been so dedicated and had volunteered their time and who had been very excited about the play understood my decision to a degree.

I went home and licked my wounds.

But in the midst of my dark solitude wherein I felt the sharp bite of betrayal and greed and anger from this other person, I had a moment of great clarity.

What if I had done this to this person in another time and place?

What if I had been in a production capacity perhaps a century or more ago and I'd had control of this person's play and become greedy, jealous, or a slew of other negative emotions that caused her to have to pull the play just as I had done?

What if it was all repeating itself, with me now dealing with a karmic debt of forgiveness that had to be repaid?

I pondered this scenario for many days and finally came to the conclusion that my thoughts were most likely spot on.

Without a moment's hesitation I sent out a message to the universe stating my sorrow for having most likely once destroyed this person's great chance at fame. I also did an email contact with her.

The story ended there, and I felt I had indeed been on the right track.

My play went into a file for several years and just recently has had some interest shown by a local theater group.

Will it ever be produced? I have no way of knowing—but I have hope.

I am very thankful that at least I have had the thrill and validation of almost seeing something I wrote come to life on the stage, and that is much more than many others get in this lifetime.

In the end, this interaction was all about recognizing my past-life role in another person's disappointment, and then forgiving, accepting, and moving forward.

As noted, after family relationships, my worksites have always seemed the venue for the hard lessons to be learned.

Some of these re-met ones were of the most ruthless variety.

At various office positions I have met with greed, jealousy, lust, betrayal, childish behavior, and selfishness cut through with cruelty.

Other than family ties, the workplace is, to me, the next most interesting and perfect stage for past-life interactions to be worked out. Here, I have found, is an "ask no quarter, give no quarter" mentality. Often, going to the boss to complain puts one in the framework of being a petty human being—and, indeed, complaints are often laughed at or scorned, or one is seen as a mere troublemaker.

Obviously, many of the bosses I have had over the years were not enlightened souls.

I have been brought to tears, been laughed at, ridiculed, and given the cold shoulder by women I have worked with—and even in my despair I sensed a playing out of events from other times and places. After my regression sessions I knew that a power beyond my ken had definitely arranged these re-meetings precisely as they were supposed to happen for all of us to learn the lessons we were supposed to learn and also to find forgiveness and understanding.

Some years ago I was most literally forced out of a job, but again the timing for me to leave was perfect—although I didn't think so at the time. However, I still managed, despite my obviously positive choice of a full-time writing career, to carry a bit of resentment in my heart for the people who had brought me to my position of having to resign.

One day about a year or so after my leave-taking, I met up with one of my old workmates out in public. We chatted amiably for a few moments and then I looked at this person and said, "I forgive you"—and I meant it, because at that time I was moving past the hurt and into a whole new life of doing what I had always wanted to do, which was to write full-time. The person said, "Yes. I think everything worked out the way it was supposed to, and we all have gotten what we wanted." We hugged, and I immediately felt the heavy burden of that karmic debt lift from my soul.

Could it be possible that in another time and place I had somehow forced this person out of a job that was loved? It most certainly could have happened that way. But the main thrust was that I recognized this as a possibility and offered love and kindness and understanding instead of avoidance and resentment.

It wasn't easy, but, in the end, my workmate was right— we had both gotten exactly what we wanted, and between us a karmic debt had been healed and paid in full.

The Eyes Have It

I know for a fact that the eyes are the mirror of the soul— because that is one of the main ways I have recognized past-life friends, loved ones, and enemies.

When I first re-met my dear Butch in this lifetime in 1967, there was a *zing* of instant recognition on a soul level when he looked across at me and smiled. And even though neither of us had any idea of what reincarnation was, when we looked into one another's eyes for those brief moments I saw my own self—my dreams, desires, wants, and needs—all reflected there.

In fact, when Butch and I were spending our first summer together in 1968, he often came to pick me up at my home without telling any of his local relatives he was coming. We would drive way out onto back-country roads far from the interference of adults or pesky youngsters, park the car, get out, and run hand in hand through the sweet-smelling meadows to a sheltered spot. There we sat and kissed and talked for hours or just sat back to back and watched cloud formations go by. One day, Butch suggested something new, and to this day I have no idea what prompted this suggestion—except from somewhere inside his heart an incredible past-life memory rose up to the surface that neither of us had any awareness of at the time.

Butch wanted us to sit facing one another—knees touching, holding hands, foreheads together—and gaze ever so deeply into one another's eyes. At first we had a bad case of the giggles, but then the eye contact became more serious. We somehow learned during those summer days of birdsong and clear blue skies to look *soul deep*, marveling at the pupils dilating, the rings of gold around the pupils, and letting the new and powerful feelings of connecting deeply on a timeless level course through us. Again, we had no words for what we were feeling, but we played this game many times—little realizing that we had very nearly done the same thing in a long, long-ago time and place.

With our eyes shining with hope, we were forging a connection that would continue to endure for all eternity.

But, true love aside for a moment, it is really the same for most re-meetings of lovers—that nearly flickering instant of recognition that flares in the eyes is a very validating moment that cannot be denied.

Inherent in this re-meeting is intense joy and overwhelming feelings of "being back again" in the physical presence of someone you somehow already *know* on a soul level—even though at the moment of re-meeting you are both really physically strangers to one another. I liken it to being in unfamiliar surroundings and then, across the room, spying the smiling face of someone totally familiar. It is a truly comforting thing.

But then again, there are also those you may meet whose eyes you cannot or do not want to gaze into. There is something there that doesn't feel friendly or comforting or is far from joyful. I wouldn't say the feeling is evil as it pertains to the gaze of someone you meet and instantly dislike, but there is a *bad* or *unsettling* sensation that slides like an awakening dull current of electricity through the soul.

Both parties may do all they can to avoid eye contact, and this, to me, is a sure sign of re-meeting a soul that once did you wrong or that you wronged.

It is interesting to me that sometimes the narrator on a true-crime television program mentions that the criminal showed no emotion or his or her eyes were dead and cold. Not to go off on a tangent, but if you ever look into the eyes of a serviceman—or any man trained to kill—his eyes are hard and, to me, seem to be focused purely on another darker reality. The same type of eyes looks out at us when we confront a homicide detective or one who has seen the worst of man's inhumanity to man. I truly believe that those degrees of darkness carry over from one lifetime to the next and look out from the eyes.

I Look The Same?

It could happen.

There have been many documented cases of reincarnated souls reborn in bodies that closely resemble the body type, face, and so forth that they had in a previous lifetime. I have had this happen with three of my love relationships, and it is incredible validation of continuation.

It wasn't a case of reincarnation, but it illustrates the point —several years ago I happened to be dining out one evening at a local restaurant with my husband, Dan. I looked up and scanned the room and saw, seated at a table at the other end of the place, one of my favorite teachers from my elementary-school days. She was with a group of people, and as I did not want to go over and interrupt her meal, I stayed seated.

When Dan and I were finishing up our meal, she approached our table, looked at me, and said, "Marilou? It's you, isn't it? I'd recognize you anywhere. Your smile and your eyes are exactly the same as when you were in my class at Valleyview School."

After I introduced her to Dan and we spent a little while catching up on over fifty years of time, we hugged goodbye and wished one another well.

I sat down and pondered how remarkable it was that someone I hadn't seen in over a half-century *recognized* me because of my smile and my eyes!

And it is exactly like that when we re-meet someone we have known in a past life.

Certain physical attributes look familiar.

Sometimes I think that this soul return to a similar-looking physical body might happen so that the person can be more easily recognized by others in their soul circle—or perhaps the soul felt comfortable in a particular body type.

If we souls maintain our personalities, likes, dislikes, skills, and so forth when we pass to spirit, then is it really not so far-fetched to believe that we can also come back in another lifetime with the same facial features or body types?

It makes sense to me.

WHAT SKILL! WHAT TALENT!

Well, now here's a definite plus to being reincarnated.

Talents and skills usually carry over from lifetime to lifetime.

Again, I speak from personal experience.

When I was just three years of age, I yearned to re-re-learn my former abilities. The one that meant the absolute most to me was the skill of writing—of communicating with words put down on paper.

I penned my first short, short story before I was four, learned to read beyond my grade level before I entered kindergarten, and desired nothing more than to be a writer when I grew up.

And to me this skill came quite easily and naturally. I only needed the rudimentary instruction offered by my dear grandfather to kick-start my brain into speeding along merrily. I amazed my grandparents' elderly friends, who would stop by the house when I read to them from a book more in line with an older child's intelligence level—or read them the story I had written. They remarked, "Well, isn't she just the smartest little thing!"Or, "My daughter couldn't read books like that until she was much older." I took to writing and printing and forming words into sentences like the proverbial duck to water.

To me, there was nothing at all remarkable about my talent.

It was just something I could do.

As my friend Diana Kenyon wrote in the foreword to this book, there are so many children born with innate skills. Children play Mozart, paint beautiful pictures, and dance and sing at such early ages that they seem like miniature adults because their talent is mind-boggling to many.

But to those who believe in reincarnation, it is a simple fact—the child is exhibiting skills the soul within learned in another time and place.

Where do your skills and talents lie?

What gives you passion?

For some it can be a grand talent like music or acting or writing. For others it may be the art of cooking or painting or caring for children or animals, or being the best mom or dad in the world.

The valid test of a past-life skill is this: it comes very easily to you with very little effort. You may not even need any instructions at all in the chosen art or skill. Some may have been able to do the thing—play a musical instrument, write, paint—from a very early age. It is something that if you could not do it, you wouldn't know what else to do. It is your joy, your bliss, your escape from the workaday world—and one day you hope to be able to do it full-time, leaving behind the drudgery of the nine-to-five world and offering your particular talent to those eager to receive it.

An interesting thing I've found when I am fully immersed in writing is that time seems no longer to have any meaning. There is a sense of timelessness when involved in a creative project of any sort—be it painting, writing, playing a musical instrument—because therein lies peace and a connection to the you that once was and is again.

Do Pets Reincarnate?

There are many who believe that they do.

During my last near-death experience in 1984, when my guardian angel returned with me to Heaven, I saw there before me not only my loved ones who had passed to spirit but also all my sweet pets.

Later I saw these dear furry ones go by me in spirit in my home and had dream visitations from them.

I pondered that if an animal most beloved has a soul that survives physical death, then it is not too much of a leap to believe that they also reincarnate. The reason I believe this is because of the love and the bond created between many humans and their pets.

I truly believe that our present cat, Pretty, has the soul of my dear Muffin, who passed away many years ago. She has the same voice, the same caring eyes, and the very same likes and dislikes that Muffin had. I used to call Muffin my "Nurse Kitty" because if I were ill she would barely leave my side except to eat, drink, and use the litter box. Her furry presence was always nearby, snuggled up against my body and offering such great comfort and compassion. She had the habit of reaching out with her paw and very gently touching my cheek as if to make sure I was okay. No cat since Muffin has exhibited that particular behavior. All of these things are manifest in this dear cat that came to us out of nowhere just before our sweet Quincy passed to spirit about two years ago.

As I don't believe in coincidence in any way, this is validation to me that I am dealing with the reincarnation of my dear Muffin, the cat I called "Wee Weege" and who responded to that pet name just as Pretty does.

Again, prefacing this incident with my non-belief in coincidence, there is also this story:

About fifteen or so years ago, Dan and I were overrun with feral cats. The population zoomed upwards of twenty or more at a time, and we fed them all as best we could. Gradually their population dwindled due to their tragic deaths on the road in front of the house and, we believe, a bit of poisoning done by humans. In any event, we were down to only about four or five.

One day a large yellow tomcat showed up. He was much harassed by neighbor children, who often shot at him and missed. But one day he came close to using up all of his nine lives when two dogs, which had been left to run wild, chased him into the yard. One had his tail, and the other was intent on making a meal out of him. I was in the kitchen, saw what was happening, and called for Dan, who went out and chased the dogs away. The set-upon cat was hiding underneath one of the sheds on our property. We were unable to see him to assess his wounds and, as darkness was coming on, had to leave him in the relative protection of the building.

After that day we never saw him again and, even though we looked, his body was nowhere to be found.

He had simply vanished or gone off to live elsewhere or to die in solitude.

Fast forward fifteen years, and as if out of nowhere another lithe yet scroungy-looking yellow tomcat appears in nearly the same area of the shed that we saw the other one! He has the same mannerisms, same build, and same face—yet he is somehow altered in disposition and craves the attention and love we give him. He is ensconced in comfort in our now-heated garage with his special bed, blanket, toys, food, and water, and is cared for tenderly.

Could he be the reincarnation of the tom that was here years ago?

I believe he is.

Could I Reincarnate as an Animal?

Some people or religions do believe that this happens, but it is not something I have ever had any experience with—yet it is a question I am occasionally asked when the question-and-answer period of one of my public speeches about the dead veers off to the topic of reincarnation.

I suppose I believe that in the end, coming back as one of my pet cats or dogs or a bird might give me a flight of fancy for a few moments—but deep in my own soul I truly believe that humans come back in human form and animals, birds, etc., in their own forms.

Still, it is interesting to consider.

This Place Seems Very Familiar!

That incredible, goose-pimply feeling you might get when you visit an absolutely new place and yet feel that it is somehow familiar—as if you had been there before—is called déjà vu. It has happened many times for me, even as a young child visiting historical places. In my book *Dreaming of the Dead*, I describe the overwhelming sensation of déjà vu that came over me the first time I visited actor/playwright William H. Gillette's castle home in Connecticut. That was an absolutely remarkable experience, as I was able to know on a soul level that certain aspects of the home had changed since Mr. Gillette died in 1937 and, more importantly, to point out those things correctly.

This sensation of intense familiarity can happen with people or situations or even conversations. There have been many occasions in my life when I have been talking with someone perhaps recently met to whom I feel a connection, and an overwhelming sense of *I've done this before with this person* comes over me. Sometimes I mention it aloud, but most often I acknowledge the feeling and continue with the discussion.

Déjà vu brings an incredible and comforting sense of connectedness to a place never before visited in this lifetime—or to a person, an event, even a pet—and allows a glimmer of thought to enter the mind that reincarnation is very real and that the place or situation we have found ourselves in was a part of a previous lifetime.

BIRTHMARKS AND BIRTH DEFECTS

When I was still young, about ten or so, I remember being out at a grocery store with my grandparents and seeing a child with a huge, reddish-purple mark that covered one side of his face. The "stain," as Grandpa called it, was most odd because it seemed to have pointed edges to it that reminded me of flames. Recalling that child after I underwent my regression sessions in my mid-thirties, I began to wonder if perhaps that soul in that body had indeed died by fire and that the death had been so painful and traumatic that it had not only scarred the body but also the soul.

Similar cases have been reported of children who are the reincarnated souls of those killed in a war being reborn with a bullet-shaped indentation at the point where they were shot and killed in another time.

Birth defects are along the same lines. Many babies are born with missing fingers or toes or misshapen limbs. Dr. Stevenson found during his past-life research that these defects matched exactly with a past-life trauma carried over into the present lifetime.

What a powerful hold on our souls tragedy and trauma in other lives inflicts.

Could Knowing My Past Lives Heal Me?

Again, I can only speak from personal experience, but I'd say yes. Knowing who and what you were in another time and place could definitely give insight into fears, phobias, illnesses, and so forth.

For example, as you will read in later chapters about my regression sessions, I believe that the panic/anxiety attacks I manifested during this lifetime had a lot to do with one of my past lives. Another past life I had may have been the true beginning of my asthmatic condition in this incarnation, and, most definitely, my absolute terror of childbirth was also rooted in a past-life experience.

Thankfully, my asthma was healed by angelic intervention. I didn't really have to deal with the fear of childbirth in this lifetime as I had made a conscious decision to remain childless when I was about four. The panic and anxiety attacks ceased after I came to peace with their source and let go of fear-based thinking. It is a definite fact that my regression session that rooted out the source of the dis-ease was of great help to me in healing.

Parental/Family Influence

One of the ways that skeptics discount the past-life memories of children is to state that the child must have overheard adults talking about an event, place, or person and committed this bit of information to memory. So, when a very young child, usually about the age of two or three, begins talking about being a grandfather or great-aunt or another family member in another time and place—well, eyebrows are raised. And when the child can even pick out relations, homes, pets, and so forth from photos without any supposed prior knowledge, naysayers will consistently state that the child merely overheard the adults talking.

Again, I can only draw from my own personal experience with this.

As an infant being raised by my Irish Catholic grandfather and my sweet, Southern Baptist grandmother in a small, rural community in upstate New York, I would not have heard discussions about ancient Egypt during the reign of any particular pharaoh, about medieval laundresses at Welsh castles, or elements of any of the other lifetimes I was regressed to in my mid-thirties.

My grandparents were of the hardworking, simple stock of immigrant and family native to this soil. Grandpa's favorite topics of conversation when I was growing up were more likely to be garden seeds, ordering baby chicks, and his work on the railroad or at a local hospital as a custodian. He did often speak about his life in Ireland and his belief in ghosts, leprechauns, and pixie folk, but those subjects did not come through in my past-life regression sessions.

Grandma was also knowledgeable about chicks and seeds, but her favorite topics were her home state of South Carolina and her family there. Religion was important to both of them. Again, during my regression sessions I never found that I had lived a lifetime in South Carolina. Never do I recall either of them sitting with me at the supper table and talking about distant times—they simply had no interest in such things. The immediate future and the present moment were of the utmost importance to them, as they had to plan in advance for the coming seasons of the year. Having lived through the Great Depression, they knew the value in that planning and had no interest in ancient times.

To my grandparents, ancient history had little to do with putting food in the house or making money from not only Grandpa's job but also from the selling of eggs from our chickens and the plentiful vegetable garden.

Ancient Egypt was never in their thoughts.

There is also another part of the parental thing that I must bring forward, and that is the parents who de-validate a child's imagination. Many children, me included, have or had imaginary friends—well, I didn't have imaginary people friends; I had to be different. I had imaginary animal friends. My first imaginary animal friend was a rabbit I named "Hopper," and he was a grayish-brown adult rabbit. I could see Hopper perfectly well. He followed me everywhere and slept by the side of my bed at night. This was when I was about four and just coming into my own and communicating with ghosts on a pretty regular basis. One day I was outside talking aloud to Hopper, and Grandpa happened by. "Who are you talking to, Johnny?" (Johnny was his tomboy nickname for me), he asked.

I simply replied, "My pet rabbit Hopper." Grandpa leaned down, and I almost believe to this day that he was seeing the rabbit for himself.

"That's a good-looking rabbit you've got there. Does it eat much?" This was something I hadn't thought of. "How about we go up to the garden and get it a carrot and make it up a nice bed to sleep in?"

Well, I was all for that! Hopper and I followed Grandpa up to the garden, where he pulled up a nice ripe carrot that he washed off in the little stream by the baby-chick coop. Then we went to the garage for a cardboard box. Grandpa pulled some grass for the box and cut the carrot up into small pieces with his jackknife and put the pieces in the box. I looked down and saw that Hopper was sitting there beside me watching everything closely. Grandpa put the box on the ground and told me to have Hopper jump in. I did so, and the rabbit was soon in the box.

Grandpa carried the box down to the house and put it beside my bed. Every day Grandpa and I would put in some fresh grass or ripped-up newspaper and something for Hopper to eat, throwing out the pieces he didn't finish. Hopper was one contented rabbit. My invisible rabbit and I had about a year together, and he vanished a few days after I started kindergarten.

The point of this is that my grandfather—make that my very wise grandfather—never once told me that Hopper was "all in my imagination" or to "stop being so silly" and so forth. He totally engaged with me, and I still recall how exciting it was to be able to share Hopper with him. Grandpa encouraged me to have an imagination, and despite my schoolteachers, clergy, friends, neighbors, and other family members who did tell me to "stop that" or gave me those sideway, odd looks, I always clung to the fact that my grandpa never took from me the most valuable gift of all—imagination.

That Chance Meeting

This was such an incredible occurrence in my life that I feel I must share it here, because it is exactly the way most re-meetings happen.

One summer day in the mid-1970s—and before the word *reincarnation* was part of my vocabulary—I was walking down a sidewalk in New York City. The DO NOT WALK sign flashed, and I stopped with a group of other pedestrians. When we were at last able to cross the street and get on the sidewalk, an odd thing happened to me. I felt as if a momentous occasion were about to occur. There was a nearly electrical energy zinging through me and a trembling in my body. My heart rate quickened slightly. As I was drawn forward by the surge of other bodies all eager to get to their destinations, my attention was drawn to my left.

The air seemed to nearly pulsate with anticipation from some unknown source.

For reasons unknown to me, I hesitated in my forward journey.

Coming toward me with a purposeful stride was a blond-haired man of about thirty or so. He was very clean-cut and wearing a tan suit, and he was carrying a briefcase. He and I came even with one another, and we both paused and gazed into one another's eyes—his were the most remarkable deep blue. For that infinitesimal moment the hurrying people around us seemed to vanish as if they didn't exist and time stood still. I heard no sounds of traffic, saw no one else but this one man, and I believe he experienced the same. Though he was a complete stranger, we *knew* one another deeply and intimately—or had in some other time and place.

We never spoke.

Then I was pushed into by someone who was probably annoyed with my standing in the pathway, and the spell was broken. The man moved forward, and so did I. We glanced back at one another quickly and then continued walking away from one another.

To this day I don't know why one of us didn't attempt to speak.

Was it the shock of re-meeting perhaps?

Certainly, now looking back at the experience, the precise timing of the powers that control such meetings was right on.

If I had been a few moments sooner or later, or if he had, perhaps that meeting would not have happened.

But if there was no future in the relationship, why did we meet that day?

Did we only need to reconnect briefly to see that one another was okay?

And the question I ponder to this day—who was he?

For a while I wondered if he might have been an angel, because his eyes so reminded me of my own guardian angel who had healed me on two occasions in my life.

I pondered it then and do now. It was as if all the emotions of a lifetime were lived between us in those few moments— love, passion, desire, concern, joy, and finality.

It is a mystery that, at least in this lifetime, may never be solved.

But it was very obvious that we were, or had been, very important to one another at least on a soul level.

Whoever or whatever he was, the entire experience was surreal, and I never knew exactly how long it lasted in actual time. However long it was, the experience was imprinted on my soul forever.

And it was another defining moment in my life that would echo forward in time during my meeting with my mentor and therapist about ten years in the future.

Chance, random, coincidental meetings are anything but.

Like all meetings, it was perfectly timed.

I mean, what are the odds that I would be walking down a sidewalk in New York City on that precise day and time to see this man? The odds must be a zillion to one—yet there we both were.

I have never had an experience exactly like that since.

But when you really think about it, all meetings are by chance—or perfectly planned, or at least I believe they are—by a power beyond our ken that times it all so perfectly.

My handsome New York City man is just an example. Perhaps we were not supposed to have a relationship this lifetime. Perhaps we only needed to touch base for a brief moment because we had done it all before and perfectly.

But one thing I do know for certain: there is no such thing as a chance meeting.

Another personal observation: to me, reincarnation, like my near-death experiences and communications with those who have passed to spirit, offers not only incredible proof of, but also deep comfort about, the continuity of life.

REINCARNATION AND DESTINY

Some may wonder if all the deeds done in another lifetime impact their present-day lives, and I would have to say this is definitely true. There is no escaping from the wheel of life as it turns onward from the past to the present to the future. The idea is to be able to pay off karmic debt and get off the wheel of rebirth. Otherwise, we cannot help but repeat patterns that we had in other times and places. It may, at times, take a conscious effort to bring this about.

What habits, personality traits, character flaws, and positive attributes make up the sum total of who you are now? This honest self-assessment will give you clues as to what needs to be worked on this time around.

When I did this bit of past-life detective work, I simply sat down with a notebook, made two columns, and listed what I felt my positive and not-so-positive character traits were. After my regression sessions I had a clearer view of who I had been in my past lives and what traits had come through with me to this lifetime. It was a revelation to me, to be sure. And, as I said, without fail I found that my past lives and my present life pretty much parallel one another in regard to these traits. I had been interested in learning new things then and still am. I had been a writer and contemplative and have those traits to this day.

It is all so very interesting and marvelous to truly know yourself.

Chapter Two

FINDING MY WAY BACK

On brilliant sunshiny days in the summer of my third year, I used to rush out of the house in the mornings after a hearty breakfast of oatmeal or eggs and toast and fresh-squeezed orange juice to go and sit on the wooden-seated rope swing my grandfather had put up for me on a limb of the lawn maple that resided in the front yard. That swing seemed to be a place where I could be transported into realms of thought that loosened my soul and allowed it to soar beyond the confines of Earth's most restrictive barriers.

After I got my momentum going, I always leaned as far back as I could while maintaining a very tight hold on the rough rope with both hands. I put my head back and gazed up through the canopy of green leaves, allowing the back-and-forth motion of the swing to soothe me into a nearly drowsy state. Then I closed my eyes and waited.

It wasn't long before I began to feel totally free of the confines of Earth and as if I were above the clouds with my sights turned toward the place my child self called *home*.

During these early childhood days, the feeling often washed over me that this place I called *home* was truly a realm unseen by earthly eyes. Although it was a haven of love and kindness, it definitely was not the sweet little bungalow named Pleasant View that I lived in with my beloved grandparents—the two who had been my parents since I was a newborn.

No.

I felt that this other *home* was far more unique than a building made of wood and nails bound by the love of the two who were not related by blood to me but instead joined by hearts entwined in a circle of caring.

This real *home* of mine was of a more ethereal quality, and there resided so many I had left behind in order to be present here at this particular time. Then there was the very puzzling perception that I had lived in many different earthly homes in other places far distant from here—knowledge I'd had since I was a tiny baby lying in Grandma's arms.

I opened my eyes slightly and looked at my strong and slim legs kicking upward toward the heavens and had the fleeting thought that my body was also a home. It was a very odd thought but somewhat comforting. I brought back to me the knowledge that I had been in bodies before and that each one had been a new beginning for me.

I closed my eyes again and kept kicking skyward.

The leaves above me swished as the ropes of the swing brushed against them, and the movement caused myriad patterns of sunlight to dapple my eyelids.

Memories came to me—fast flashes and dazzling sensations engulfed me.

Memories of my present-day infanthood cascaded once more through my mind. I recalled the time when I had tried so desperately to get to this point in my life, when I could once again run and play and talk. I recalled the days just after my revelations at age three months, and the desperation I had felt at not being able to control my hand movements or to communicate with my grandparents by speech—which I had totally understood as an infant but aggravatingly could not utilize.

I recalled a trying time in all our lives when it was told to me by my grandparents that I was very nearly kidnapped and sold as an infant, and through the quick thinking of my grandfather I returned to my much-loved Pleasant View. My developing senses had been reawakened by the tenseness and the fear that had encompassed that nearly tragic day and event. My grandfather gave me no other details other than outlining who was involved in this horrendous scheme. I had solid memories of my grandmother weeping, a fast car ride home from the place where I had been held, and once back at Pleasant View the sight and sound of shades being drawn as we waited in total stifling silence for a much-dreaded knock at the door that would herald the arrival of those who would take me from the loving embrace of my grandmother and grandfather and my dear, sweet home.

After this decidedly horrific event was over, I was exhausted on every level of my small being. In a very short time I had become aware of the fact that I had lived in other times and places through my reawakening, found that there was no way to recoup the abilities I knew I had once had, and I had almost been kidnapped and sold. I again made a conscious decision to shut down until I would be able to return to my former physical and verbal skills.

There was, I remembered, a brief and exciting moment when I was again cognizant of my earth age as being about ten months. My grandfather had put me on the linoleum-covered parlor floor, and he then went to sit down on the sofa and read his newspaper. Grandma kept coming in and out of the room. I recall that I got my knees pulled under me with some effort and began to push off. I didn't get very far and sort of stayed put, rocking back and forth. My brain urged me forward, but I could not accomplish the thing. After many tiring moments, I pushed my legs back and lay on my stomach and began crying, and Grandpa came and picked me up.

A few weeks later, I finally succeeded when I again got on my knees and realized I had to put one hand in front of the other and also move my legs. I was off at last—able to crawl and take an exciting first movement toward independence. Such a feeling of freedom this movement allowed me! I was so proud of myself, and I remember that my grandparents gave me many hugs and kisses of congratulations.

But I craved more.

Once I mastered crawling, my mind urged me onward to greater things.

One day my grandmother stood me up and held onto me. My legs were a bit wobbly, but I thought that if I could lock my knees I wouldn't topple forward. Now I was feeling almost powerful and knew that it was at last time to use my legs to walk upright, as I had done so many times before in other bodies.

Grandma took me down the bedroom hallway. She held my hand as we moved up and down along the brief corridor. I kept one hand on the wall. I pushed off on one foot and felt it hold my weight. I remember looking down at my feet a lot, amazed that I was gaining more control of my body. Grandma's firm grip kept me moving. At last I was able to stand upright again, and I was both exhausted and exhilarated by the experience!

This was the moment I had been waiting for—well, at least one of them.

Now I wanted to learn to talk better and read and write.

So, I bided my time until I was about two years of age and found that I could once again speak a few words to make my needs known. I could run—sometimes falling, but always picking myself up and feeling joy that my body was at last working the way it was supposed to again.

Since the time I had been about one year old, my grandparents had been reading to me every day. I remember sitting on Grandpa's lap and him taking my tiny finger and tracing it over the words in the books he read aloud to me each night before bedtime. My brain was totally comprehending that he was speaking aloud the words I was touching, and I soon recognized some of the simpler ones, like *the* and *it* and so forth.

During the latter part of my second year, my grandfather began a new nightly ritual. After supper was over, the table cleared, and the dishes washed and put away, he would sit and tutor me in writing and arithmetic, shapes and colors and pictures. This was all done on the white, metal, pull-out top of our kitchen buffet. Prior to each lesson Grandpa always sharpened a pencil stub with his jackknife before handing it to me. Every night was a different lesson, and so by the time I was nearing my third year, I could easily recite the alphabet, recognize many words, and write my name and address. I could also add and subtract, and by the time I was four I would know how to make change for a twenty-dollar bill.

With only a second-grade education, my grandfather had given me the next most precious gift of my life—knowledge—and I ate it all up, being very thankful that this dear, hardworking man knew on some soul level that I was eager and needed his help.

Again, I knew I had been placed in exactly the right home and with the right people who could help me on my path.

Despite the fact that the process was painstakingly slow, and I often felt that so much valuable time was being wasted on relearning skills I had already achieved in other times, I was finally coming back to me!

By the time I was three I actually felt anger, because of all the time I'd had to waste to return to my former abilities of speech and walking and writing and all the rest. And this was actually the age I penned my first short, short story (with Grandpa's help) titled "The Little Hurt Bird." This was the story of a baby robin Grandpa had found injured alongside the road in front of our home. Together we nursed it back to health. This was also the age I became totally fascinated with copying material from Grandpa's Nash Rambler car manual—or any other book I found intriguing. Little did I know that even this act was an echo of a past life that would be revealed to me some thirty years or so in the future.

Now, swinging back and forth and experiencing the joy of being me again, yet somehow because of all the learning I had done in the last few years, I let the remembering go deeper.

Although I had no real people or events to put together with my thoughts, I knew that during my other times here on Earth that I had always yearned for that glorious place called *home*. I knew that in that place there had been clouds and blue skies and meadows that went on endlessly toward a golden horizon—the place I knew I returned to after each time on Earth. I thought about the me that used to be, and I truly felt that I had been very blessed to have lived in those different bodies and known all the people I had known in those times in the past. Some memories were beautiful— some not so much. I knew I had experienced deep and abiding true love and the loss of that love on quite a few occasions. I had been born and died and then returned to start all over again. I had been a part of the lives of the same people during a few of my returns. I had witnessed the deaths of beloved family and friends and pets and had suffered deeply from those losses—yet somehow and for some reason I knew I had returned to experience it once more.

I allowed the swing to slow, and I got off and walked up the hill to sit by the baby-chick coop. Grandpa was home, hoeing in the garden, and Grandma was in the house preparing lunch.

At age three I stood teetering on the brink of discovery and embraced it all. It came to me that this time things were a bit different because this was a life I had somehow *chosen* and not one that had been chosen for me, as I knew all the other ones had been. I also knew that in that choosing there was both freedom and responsibility. I understood somehow that my soul had progressed far enough on its journey that I had been allowed to request a return to Earth at this precise time in history and to this living situation with the two I knew as my grandparents. All of this knowing left me with feelings both powerful and frightening. I sensed that the beings that I had made this momentous request of still resided in this place called *home* and that they were compassionate, stern yet fair, and extremely ancient.

As summer turned to autumn, I spent more time mentally descending into the zone where I let go of my attachment to the physical form I was now inhabiting and allowed a few of my past-life place scenes to glide through my mind. I observed each one closely, looking for clues that would point me in the right direction for this sojourn on Earth. And although a lot of what I was viewing in my mind's eye didn't make a lot of sense, I knew it was important for me to connect with it for the future. I also found that as I descended more deeply into my long-ago past that I yearned even more to return to my true *home*, and for a short span of time this obsession with the place became a secret desperation that engulfed my young self causing me to often stop whatever I was doing quite abruptly and run up the meadow path to the forest and climb to the top of a gigantic oak.

Once there I would reach skyward—imploring whatever force had left me here to come immediately and take me back. I had caught a quick mental glimpse of one of my past lives play out, and it dealt with anguished, pain-filled crying. I saw no images but knew that the woman screaming in agony was me in another time and place, and the sounds scared me deeply. From this I knew that earthly life came with certain joys but also with pain and heartache, and I shrank away from the tears and the grieving I knew would be my lot.

When no answer or help came and I discerned deeply the vast silence from that other dimension, I gave up and resigned myself to staying put.

Because I knew that I had no real choice.

There was something larger and more powerful than my simple desires at work here, and I had to obey the dictates that had been laid down for this particular chosen soul journey.

As I climbed reluctantly down from the tree and began trudging homeward, my very young self now realized there would be no turning back.

It wasn't long after the summer of my third year that the life lessons began for me.

During the winter of 1954 I became very ill with pneumonia and was hospitalized. During that hospital stay I had my first near-death experience, wherein I was briefly allowed admittance to that most coveted place—Heaven or *home*. When I arrived there, I was led by the spirit of a young girl named Emmie—who appeared to be about five to six years of age and from another time period, judging by her clothing. Emmie did her absolute best to lure me back and have me stay with her and a group of children playing in a sunlit meadow in what I recognized as my true home. But I found I was not as willing or wanting to return as I had once so desperately wished a few months prior.

In my very ill state, I clung to the hope of going home to Pleasant View and my grandparents' loving hearts. It was also during this time that I made the acquaintance of my guardian angel—a beautiful young man with long, wavy brown hair and incredibly compassionate blue eyes—who stayed close by me at the hospital. This was such a comfort, as he was at least a being I recognized from my ethereal *home*. On the day I woke up in the hospital, the angel healed me with the gentle touch of his hand on my forehead.

This first near-death experience is what I believe opened a portal in my young soul and allowed me communication with those on the other side of life's doorway.

By the spring of my fourth year, I was in communication with spirits who came to me in form. During my late teen years, these visitations switched over, and the dead began coming to me in very vivid dreams—only rarely making appearances in form.

In 1967, during the summer of my sixteenth year, four things happened almost simultaneously. First, I met and fell deeply in love with the tall, slim, brown-eyed boy who I would later find had been a part of my past-life vision when I was three months old—the one who had resided with me in that beautiful city of temples and sea breezes. We met at exactly the right time in both our lives, and the recognition was complete when we looked into one another's eyes. It was a pure and innocent love that would solidify the eternal bonding of our souls to an even greater degree and depth when he passed to spirit about twenty years after our reunion.

Just prior to this incredible re-meeting with Butch, I had three other miracles occur: a near-death experience, a healing from my guardian angel, and dreams of great import. My guardian angel came to me while I was having an asthma attack in my bedroom at Pleasant View. This event catapulted me into the near-death experience, and when I returned to my body the angel cured me of my asthma by once more laying his hand gently on my forehead and telling me I was healed. After a remarkably wonderful night's sleep— the best I'd had in quite a while—I woke up the next morning thinking it had all been a dream. I felt as if *something* inside—deep, deep inside—had altered. I felt an almost familiar lightness of being that gave me the knowledge that I was no longer the person I had been a few short hours prior. I knew then in my heart that I had not dreamed the angel's visit, but had been in the presence of that heavenly guide and that a miracle had once more happened in my life. I felt so truly blessed and very grateful.

Later that day I would test the theory and go up back to the meadow and run and run—something I could not have done in the past without bringing on a dreaded asthma attack. I stopped and waited for the squeezing, suffocating feeling in my throat and chest to come. But it didn't. The angel had healed me, and I was once again whole and ready to move forward with my life as a normal teenager who was so very ready to begin a marvelous new life that was illness-free! No more would I be plagued by the horrible chronic and debilitating disease that had destroyed my life for the last ten years.

Gratefully and humbly, I stood alone in the sunshine of the summer meadow above Pleasant View and bowed my head in thankfulness to my guardian angel who had made the journey from Heaven to Earth to heal me.

Joy and freedom had returned to my life with this healing, and I ran down the hill to the embrace of my grandmother. On the way, I passed Grandpa, who was hoeing in the garden. He lifted his tan cap and paused to smile at me. I always think he knew that a miracle had happened, but he never spoke of it to me. It was as if we shared a secret about the healing.

Two days later I threw away my asthma inhaler and felt the absolute freedom of no longer having to rely on it to keep me breathing. Shortly after this at a doctor's appointment, my physician examined me after my grandmother told her, "She hasn't had an attack in a long time."

My doctor looked at me strangely, then said, "I don't know what happened to you, Marilou, but I think you are a miracle."

A few weeks after the doctor appointment, my friend Sherry said to me, "Mary, you're not using your inhaler anymore." It was a statement, not a question. I simply looked at her and said, "I don't need it anymore."

Also during the summer of my sixteenth year, I had two powerful dreams: one of the distant past and one of the future—this dream of the future was actually my first dream of premonition. The first dream, of the distant past, had me waking up gasping for breath as I felt myself drowning in a sea gone mad with crashing waves and monstrous groans and cracks, as the earth was seemingly torn in half. I was a young man, about twenty or so, and I was going down under the waves for the second time when a boat pulled alongside me and a man's hand with a black onyx signet ring on the third finger reached over the side of the vessel. I grabbed this lifeline and clung to it as hard as I could, but it was no use and the waves pulled me under. The last thing I remember was that ring and the man's oh-so-familiar blue eyes gazing at me with incredible love and sorrow.

I knew I would remember that ring and those eyes forever.

The second dream—the one of the future—found me seated on a summertime hillside surrounded by a field of daisies, lush green grass, and plentiful sunshine. A young man came up the hill toward me, but because the sun was shining so brightly from behind me, he appeared as a darkened shadow. I shaded my eyes. His face remained in the shadows, yet I could plainly see that he was wearing a red flannel shirt and faded jeans. He had somewhat curly blond hair, beautiful blue eyes, and was about six feet tall.

I knew that this person was someone I had known in another time, yet unmet during this lifetime, who would someday play a significant role in my life in the future. The overwhelming sense of "unfinished business" between us clung to the fading vision, and I also knew that the relationship had been and would be of a romantic nature—something cut short in my distant past that would be allowed completion.

Almost fifteen years to the day of that dream I would meet the man, and he was wearing the exact outfit I had seen in the dream! He and I would be married and spend six wonderful years together before divorcing. I sensed that he and I had known one another sometime in the 1800s, and quite possibly he was a Civil War soldier I had loved and who had died before we had gotten a chance to fulfill our lives together. This intense yet brief time we were together was, like all the other relationships I was to have, a way for an interrupted journey of two souls who had once loved deeply to be completed.

Later, during a regression session, I would be proven correct about the Civil War connection.

As my life progressed forward, I found that it was not always the duration of a relationship that marked its success, but the fact that the relationship was given back so that it could be completed during this lifetime—as if some incredibly benevolent force had made it so that I was reborn into a particular time with all my lost loves that allowed the continuation and the finding and the completion of what had never been finished in other lifetimes. Therefore, the end of any time together with a re-re-found love was not a negative thing but an ascertaining that our time together was simply over and the lessons that these people he and I had been were over, and it was time to move on for all concerned.

Each end signaled a new beginning and another step forward on my life path, and though saying goodbye to love brought pain and tears, it also brought a certain kind of joyful peace, knowing that we'd had that precious time granted to us and that we had loosened the ties for all of us to move forward and continue our spiritual growth as we progressed along on our now individual soul journeys.

Of course, having said that, it must also be noted that some reunions with those from my past lives were not always joyful. Many relationships I have encountered during this lifetime were fraught with anger, bitterness, sadness, jealousy, and remorse. These relationships were the ones that really needed the work, and I swiftly learned that buying into the same angst I had experienced with these re-met souls from other times would probably cast an echo into my future lives as well as theirs, and bind me to those I had no desire to meet again. The problem was that it was all too easy to get caught up in the turmoil and buy into their particular torments and thus sink to their level of soul development. It was apparent to me that many of my past lives had been darkened by the shadows of jealousy, betrayal, and abandonment. So whenever I encountered a particularly difficult person in my present life who exhibited these undesirable traits, I made every effort to draw back and try to view the situation and the world through their eyes.

Not such an easy thing to do.

Because I knew that these people had once hurt me deeply.

As I noted previously, it was almost easier to go to their level and return like for like—and I am ashamed to admit that I often did just that, especially when I was younger and didn't understand karmic debt or the ideal of forgiveness. It was such a chore to attempt to go beyond the facade these teachers (for that is exactly what they were) presented to me and try to find a modicum of goodness in them.

Then one day I heard a phrase that stuck with me. It was something like "We dislike most in others what we are ourselves."

It was an eye-opener and a difficult theory for me to accept on any level of my being.

It meant admitting that I was as flawed as the negative person impacting my life. It meant accepting that this most difficult person was in my life for a reason and knowing that they wouldn't be a part of my life if that wasn't true.

It took me a long time to accept that sentence I had heard and put it into practice, but I did it.

Because to me, these re-meetings of the negative ones from my past lives was the dealing out of karma—that eternal cycle of retribution that we build up with others over the centuries and lifetimes spent together. This led me to the very uncomfortable thought and understanding that I had quite possibly done to this other person what they were now doing to me. There are other theories about karma, but to me it was simply payback—reaping what I had sown or the echo of that old adage my grandparents and my first true love had lived by: *what goes around comes around*. It meant having to experience the emotions that I had probably once inflicted on another— it gave me a real taste of how treating others badly could influence my present life on every level and probably any future lifetimes I might have. Karmic debt: it meant paying back, righting the wrong, balancing the books, saying I was sorry and meaning it from a heart level, learning my lesson, and, most of all, forgiving not only the others but also myself.

It took so many years to learn, and to this day I still often struggle with it.

Yet time is most often a benevolent healer. The lessons I have learned from being hurt echo in my soul, and each debt paid and released with love and honest, heartfelt forgiveness brings purer hope for returning *home* one day with a much lighter burden on my soul.

Chapter Three

WHEN THE STUDENT
IS READY

It has always been a firm belief of mine that we meet exactly who we are supposed to meet at precisely the right (or even the wrong) time. Indeed, if, as some believe, the entire world is a stage, then the people who come to be a part of our lives are players who enter and exit our days as if on cue.

This is not something I truly understood until one day in the mid-1980s, just about a year or so after I was involved in a near-fatal car accident. This car accident again brought me into contact with my guardian angel, who took me on a journey to the other side of life's door and brought me into the presence of my loved ones, both human and animal, that had passed over. This was the *home* I remembered, and there I saw and felt the beauty and the unconditional love, joy, and peace that awaits us when our earthly life is over.

The angel had sent me back to my physical body with the admonition that I could not "stay" there in paradise because my "work on Earth was not yet done."

There was a mission to complete.

This was the echo of the knowing I had experienced as an infant as I lay in my grandmother's arms on that long-ago late summer day—the angel had now confirmed for me what I had felt all this time. My destiny had been validated by this most recent near-death experience, and I faced the future more steadfastly with firmer intentions.

It was time for the next teacher to enter my life.

Synchronistic events were about to occur in my life, events that would eventually turn me away from the established life I had led—a life that had kept blinders on my eyes and bound my soul to believing in limitations and following the safe way of thinking and living. In a matter of weeks I would come to believe a new adage: "Do not go where the path may lead; go instead where there is no path and leave a trail."

So it was that in the spring of 1985, just before my thirty-fourth birthday, I took a job as a secretary/receptionist at a local office. A while after I was hired, a woman joined the office team. As it seemed that my last near-death experience had made me more sensitive to the vibrations of others, I immediately felt, upon shaking her hand, the all-encompassing feelings of peace and love throughout my being. Whenever I was near her, I felt as if I were in the presence of my guardian angel—such were the feelings of charisma, comfort, and kindness that flowed around her energy field and soothed me as well as the clientele we dealt with on a daily basis.

She seemed to move within a force field of pure love and appeared outwardly to be relatively unaffected by the near chaos that often came upon our days. Indeed, it was as if she was a physical part of her surroundings and yet set apart from them.

Then came the day when I experienced one of her remarkable talents—something I had never known of before and have never experienced since. I was having some neck and shoulder pain, the remnants of the whiplash injury I had gotten during my car accident. In those first years after the accident, all I needed to do was sleep wrong, and I woke up in pain. She noticed that I was hurting and came out to my desk and told me that she was going to help me heal by using the energy in her hands to balance my energy. This form of healing was definitely okay with me, as I was never one to rely on medicines prescribed by physicians. She told me to relax, and as she positioned herself behind me she began to move her hands over the area of my body that was feeling the most discomfort. Her hands hovered a few inches above the painful area, and she never once touched me.

Amazingly and within moments, the sensations of cold and heat coursed through my clothing to my skin as if her hands themselves were alternating between being a heating pad and an ice pack. It was just what I needed. A few moments later I stood up and moved about and found that the pain was totally gone—and it never recurred again.

She explained to me that she had been told by family members as a very young child that she had the power to heal.

Later this amazing ability was confirmed by a psychic—and, despite me having no knowledge at the time what a psychic was, I believed her because the proof was in my pain-free body!

A few days after this, she began to tell me of the use of herbal remedies, foods, and juices that had healing properties. I read many of the books she had recommended and learned about homeopathic medicine and so much more.

Every person has what has been termed "defining moments"—those few minutes or even seconds when a word or phrase or event occurs that can change the course of a life.

I was about to have such a moment.

My learning was accelerating, and the path ahead was beginning to glimmer with hope. I knew I was in the presence of someone very important to me, and I resonated to her teachings and her gentle demeanor.

Several weeks passed, and we worked together smoothly on office business and while so doing began to become closer friends. One day I was in her office, and she asked to see the palms of my hands. I had no idea why she wanted to do this, but I let her look. She was very quiet as she took my hands in hers and turned and observed them closely. She seemed to be searching for something. She gently turned my hands one way and another, and then she looked into my eyes with her soft and dreamy gray-blue ones and said very calmly, "You are a very old soul, Marilou. You have come back to teach, but you are very tired. Do you feel the need to sleep a great deal?"

I responded in the affirmative, as sleep was indeed something I had craved since infanthood. Slowly I drew my hands back from hers and must have given her a quizzical look. Of course, the old-soul thing was something I did not know about—but the mention of it had struck a distant chord in my mind. She smiled at me kindly and then said, "And you have had a lifetime in Atlantis as well. If you look at your left hand, you can clearly see the mark of Atlantis on your palm."

I looked at the myriad of lines on my hand but didn't see anything out of the ordinary. Then she again took my hand in hers and traced her fingernail carefully over a distinct letter *A*. I was totally perplexed.

"What is Atlantis?" I asked.

She looked dreamily out into the distance as if she were seeing something very rare and precious in her mind's eye. "It was a beautiful city that existed about ten thousand years ago. It was a place of very advanced learning and love and harmony, although some things there did get totally out of control when power and greed began to overtake the people who lived there. It was destroyed by an earthquake and a tidal wave of gigantic proportions. Today, many people don't believe it really existed except in the imagination of the Greek philosopher Plato, who wrote about it around 350 BC." She paused. "But I know it existed, and soon you will also believe."

I must remark that at this point in time I still had not connected the vision or the dream of drowning in the cataclysm I had experienced years ago with the name Atlantis—but the connection was not too far away.

I looked at my new mentor in awe. "And my hand tells you that I was a citizen there?"

"Yes. That and quite a few other things."

"I've never even noticed the lines on my hands—not really," I said, gazing in wonderment at the many intersecting grooves both deep and fine. I tried now to find hidden messages there, but I could see nothing unusual.

"The lines on your hands tell the story of your past and your future," she said quietly, as if instructing a small child about the alphabet. "Your left hand has the traits you were born with, the right the ones you acquire." She paused before continuing. "You have a great deal to learn and in a short time. You have had many lifetimes on this earth, but this one is the one you contracted to come back for. You volunteered to return to help the earth and its people through the next phase of its growth, as so many others have done. The term for your work here is *Light Bearer*, because you will spread the light of hope throughout the world."

I sat back in my chair and looked out the window to my right. My mind was humming with what seemed like a million questions, all swirling about and making no sense at all. Yet her words had validated my extremely young knowing that I had experienced at three months—and onward to when I was sitting on my tree swing when I was very young.

Things were beginning to make an odd kind of sense.

My new mentor was speaking again. "There is a way to find out about your lifetime in Atlantis and in any other times and places you might have lived in the past, and that's called past-life regression. I'm not qualified to do that, because it really has to be done by a professional who has been certified as a hypnotherapist."

When she said the word *hypnotherapist*, I riveted my attention on her.

"You mean someone who hypnotizes you?" I asked.

"Yes. But it has to be done by a person who knows exactly what they are doing or else some pretty bad things can happen."

I felt the spiraling emotions of fear, relief, and anticipation as I sat there. It was almost too much to take in at once.

This was all so sudden—so mysterious and at the same time somewhat comforting. I had so many other things I wanted to ask, but the fact that we were in her office during a workday meant we would have to call a halt to our talk and continue it elsewhere at another time.

As if divining my thoughts, she said, "I know you probably have a lot of questions, and I will answer as many as I can for you. Just know this very old saying: 'When the student is ready, the teacher will appear.'"

I looked at her closely. She was the most unassuming of people, yet the sense of ancient power I could now feel emanating from her was tremendous.

"So, you are the teacher, and I am the student and—"

"I have come into your life at exactly the right time to teach you what you need to know to continue with your mission on Earth. When I have taught you all I can, I will leave your life and others will come to take my place to help you forward. Make no mistake, Marilou: every single person, good or bad, that comes into your life is there for a reason. There is absolutely no such thing as coincidence. It is all karmic."

I looked at her closely. "Karmic?" I asked.

She looked at her watch quickly. "A topic we will discuss soon."

Then she gazed at me lovingly, and kindness shone from her eyes. "I'm afraid your path won't be easy, Marilou. There will be skeptics and detractors and maybe even ridicule, because many of the souls of the people on Earth are asleep, and they don't want to wake up and see any other possibilities. They cling to their routines of church and daily activities, and fight being aware of their true destinies and the love and compassion and forgiveness that is to be shared among them. They don't realize that they are souls with bodies and not the other way around."

Her words made sense. How often had I as a child kept my silent counsel about the ghostly visitors I had seen or the feelings I'd had of being left here on Earth because some inner mechanism already in place in my very young mind warned me to not share the information with anyone? How often had I taken the easy path of following the rigid rules of thought laid down by society—saying the proper and right thing when my heart and soul yearned to express what I was feeling and going through. I wanted so much to experience the escape from the inflexible rules about following the proper path that wouldn't rock the boat. I now sensed that those fear-based days were nearing an end for me.

I was, I admit, somewhat uncomfortable with the new role that I was taking on—change is never easy. There was a deep sense that I was somehow betraying the doctrines I had been brought up to believe in. I knew I was now contemplating going down an unpopular path that night possibly see friends, family, and others turn their backs on me because the subjects I wanted—needed—to bring out to the world would be, for the most part, unpopular. I was scared and realized that if I allowed it, fear would be the thing that would put a roadblock in my path once more.

And I had lived with fear long enough in the form of anxiety attacks for too many years.

I had a choice.

Follow the old established path and remain asleep to the reality that was now made known to me, or go forward.

Sometime during this self-talk, I pushed fear away, squared my shoulders, and resolved to continue with courage and immense faith that none of this was a mistake. The dreams, the near-death experiences, meeting my guardian angel and having him heal me of two deadly diseases, and the meetings of various people who were there in my life as if on cue were all part of another reawakening.

This was all happening for a reason.

Echoing in my mind came the admonition of my guardian angel during my last near-death experience in 1984—the one about a mission that needed to be completed.

With great precision, the puzzle pieces of my life were beginning to click into place.

It wasn't random.

I sensed it had all been timed perfectly.

So it was that at that exact moment in that office I began to feel, on a very deep soul level, that my life had radically altered within the last few minutes and that I would never again live as if I were isolated in a shell of oblivion wherein I meandered through my days in a fog, blindly following the dictates that had been laid down for me by the confines of family, religious, or societal teachings—because those old ways of looking at life would never again resonate for me.

I had to let go totally of my old ways of living and believing. Because of this day and my time with my new mentor, my feet were now firmly on my life's path, and I no longer felt the need to hesitate because it suddenly felt right and good to have at last arrived at this point. I had been warned that it wouldn't be easy, and I accepted that. I'd tackled tough subjects before and done okay. I probably wouldn't win many popularity contests with the topics I would reveal—but again I had never sought popularity in any of my life situations.

Oddly, it felt so freeing to at last be taking these first tenuous footsteps on my true life's path. I had already been well prepared from the time of my first remembering as an infant. I'd had three near-death experiences, communicated with the dead, and been blessed with angelic healings. Like a college graduate, I had the knowledge gleaned from all the lessons I had learned, and I was now being prepared and made ready for the next phase that I knew would eventually lead to my going out into the world with my newly gained wisdom.

It was time for me to step forward with faith and leave fear behind.

That night I had the most incredibly vivid dream.

In this dream I found myself in a place of rare and unbelievable beauty and peace. I was not at all amazed by any of the things happening around me, but simply stood in the sunshine on the white stone of a large courtyard and inhaled deeply the scent of salt water and the delectable aromas of the many exotic flowers that grew in a wild array of colors all around me. I heard the cries of seagulls and shielded my eyes to look upward, and I watched them dip and glide past me as they headed off toward a huge body of water.

As far as I could see, I was surrounded by equally gleaming white buildings—some fronted with soaring columns and adorned with statues of the mythological gods I had learned about in seventh grade. The most prominent of these was Poseidon, the God of the Sea. People moved around me, almost all of them young and vibrant. Some wore long white robes and others a shorter version of the same. Some wore red uniforms and helmets—and these were both men and women. Children moved placidly past me in small groups, following behind an adult I knew was a teacher/mentor or priest. Most of those going by me wore sandals of both plain brown or beautifully detailed leather on their feet.

I looked down at myself to see if I was similarly attired and found to my amazement that not only was I clad in the same white gauzy robe and sandals, but I also knew intuitively that I was a boy—a boy of about twelve, it seemed. As I absorbed this information, I continued to look around me…the courtyard where I was standing was a sort of market square, and people were going by with baskets laden with fresh vegetables and fruits, some of which I didn't recognize. There were a great many languages being spoken, and I could understand quite a few of the unfamiliar words; that was another surprise. Men's voices shouting drew my attention to my far left, where an expanse of deep blue sea extended off into the distance. In a semicircle design, ships with billowing sails came and went after unloading their cargo.

In the further distance, mountain peaks soared heavenward, their tops obscured by slow-moving clouds.

I turned around, looked behind me, and saw there a huge building in the shape of a pyramid. I don't know why, but I thought it odd that a pyramid was in the midst of such a setting.

As I pondered this remarkable place, a tall man with startling blue eyes, wearing a white robe with a knotted rope belt, came up beside me and smiled down at me. He put his hand on my left shoulder and then, without saying a word, pointed to the top of the pyramid-shaped building.

As I watched, a huge glowing blue eye began to form there.

Then he wordlessly turned me slowly around to face him. He bent down and put his index finger in the center of my forehead. He told me to close my eyes and use my new "third eye" to see with.

I did not question him about this third eye, because I somehow divined that it was something that was a part of being a citizen here.

I did as he bid me but had a bit of difficulty adjusting my eyesight, so he told me to cover my regular eyes with the palms of my hands if I needed to.

I did and then suddenly felt the eye in the center of my forehead burn slightly and then begin to slowly open. I stood still and got control of it and found that I could see better than I ever had before—but the only problem was that everything had a sort of glowing edge to it, as if images were in a shadowy haze along their outer rims but crystal clear within. I blinked the eye, and things came into sharper focus. Incredibly, I could see for far distances. All the way across the courtyard and beyond the pyramid-shaped building, I could make out the tiniest details of a small insect crawling along a leaf on a tree that was many yards away.

This was amazing!

I took my hands away from my eyes, and as I opened them, I felt this new third eye begin to close and sort of seal itself inside my forehead. Curious, I covered my eyes again and concentrated on the third eye and felt it come back and again open. Satisfied that it was not a one-time experience, I closed it and opened my regular eyes. Using my regular eyes suddenly seemed very limiting for a few moments, but I soon got used to them again.

I looked up at the priest—for that is what I knew he was.

He smiled down at me and quietly said, "Remember this moment and remember me. We will meet again."

The scene faded away, and I woke up actually rubbing the center of my forehead where I expected the third eye to still be.

A few days later I had the opportunity to share my unusual dream with my new mentor when we met for a late lunch at a local restaurant. We had taken the afternoon off, as she had said she had so much to share with me.

Thankfully, the place we were at was relatively quiet and we were in a booth near the back of the establishment, so we had privacy and were able to talk freely.

After I had explained every detail of the dream to her, she was very quiet and seemed to choose her words carefully. "You have had another incredible experience, Marilou. Your third eye has now opened, and you will be able to see into the hearts and souls of people and situations with great clarity. This will be both a blessing and a curse, as the motives of others are not always the best. It will be up to you whether or not you share with them what you see and know. Tread carefully, because many people seek the truth but do not really want to hear it spoken aloud."

I took in the almost dire warning she had given me, as it was something I had somewhat figured out for myself prior to and after the dream. However, I was still a bit confused about the actual manifestation of the third eye. "What is this third eye? I mean, it's not really an eye like the two I have, and yet with it I was able to see for great distances."

"And you will be able to see greater distances than just the physical world around you—you will be able to gaze into the soul of the universe." Again, she paused. "The third eye. The best way to explain it in layman's terms is that it is like a portal or a doorway opening that will allow you to be more creative and intuitive. You will find that your ability to use ESP will be heightened and that visualization skills will be easily utilized."

I think I mumbled some sort of noncommittal word like "Oh," and left it at that for the time being. So much information and knowledge was overwhelming to my psyche, and it seemed that I was like someone who had not exercised in years and then taken on a full regimen of aerobics or weight-lifting. Instead of my body being sore after the workout, my mind was aching with the overload of all of the new developments in my spiritual life.

"Any other questions?" she asked.

I shook my head no.

"Now. It's time to tell you about karma." She said this while looking off at a point somewhere above my head.

She began hesitantly. "Have you ever heard the saying, 'What goes around comes around?'"

I acknowledged that I had, my mind casting quickly back in time to this being one of the rules by which my beloved Butch had lived his life and so had taught me to live mine.

"Karma is like that but on a grander soul scale. A simple explanation of karma is that it is a tally of all the good and bad things you have done over many lifetimes—so doing good will bring good things into your lifetimes, and doing bad will bring negative things"

"Who keeps this tally?" I asked.

"The universe."

"Who or what is the universe?" I asked.

She thought for a moment. "It is like all the light and love and harmonious essence of every single good person who ever lived, combined into a mind force that rules with compassion and unconditional love."

I had to ponder this for a moment and found that it made sense.

Then I had a sudden memory of something I had been taught in my early Christian upbringing about the Book of Life, wherein all the deeds done by every person were recorded and then read back or shown to a soul newly arriving in Heaven. But I had not experienced this at all during any of my three near-death experiences, so I was a bit skeptical.

I mentioned this. "I was taught in Catholic school that it was God who kept a Book of Life, and that when you died he or Saint Peter met you at the Golden Gate and did a review of your life from this book before you could enter Heaven."

My mentor smiled at me kindly and, as if she had divined my thoughts, asked, "And did you meet Saint Peter or God during any of your near-death experiences, Marilou?"

I admitted I hadn't.

"Those beliefs belong to a particular religious group. They will no longer resonate with your experiences."

"But who is the *universe*? Is it an actual person or being who exactly is recording our lives—keeping track of all the good and not-so-good things we do?" I asked.

"The universe is not a person, although it could probably take the form of one if need be—really it's a sort of collective mind force. This mind force keeps a record of everything in what are called the Akashic Records—probably what your Catholic faith referred to as the Book of Life."

I must have looked at her oddly. She went on to explain that I should think of the Akashic Records as ethereal volumes wherein automatically recorded were all the deeds of humanity since the beginning of time. *Akasha* meant "sky," and the only way to access these records was through something called astral projection—or a leaving of the soul from the body—and traveling to the dimension where the records were kept.

She spoke firmly. "Only a very few are allowed access to these sacred texts." I briefly wondered if I would ever be able to access the records. I also needed to learn more about this astral projection, but she continued speaking and I listened.

"Reincarnation and karma explain a great many of the things in this world for which no rational explanation exists," she said. "For example, they explain why one person is born into poverty and another into great wealth. Why illness befalls some and not others. Why some children are born with extraordinary talents while others struggle to read or write. Even scars are explained. A person who died in a fire or was put to death by fire in a past life might still have on their body, centuries later, red or purple birthmarks. There have been people who have been shot in another lifetime a hundred or more years ago, being reborn with an indent in the skin where the bullet entered all those years ago. You find this a lot with those souls who are being reborn from the Civil War right up to the Vietnam War."

I was, as they say, blown away by all this.

She continued. "Most of the souls who, like you, were born or seeded into Atlantis and returned to earthly life many times to teach or help others are extremely tired. You bear the burden of the centuries on your shoulders, and your souls seek to get off the cycle of birth and rebirth and return home to Source forever. Sometimes you, and these others, feel and act older than your peers, and felt this way before you were even out of diapers. When you were still a child, many adults remarked to you or to your parents that you act older than their own children. I say you are all to be commended for having the courage and the kindness of heart to want to return to help humankind through the next phase of Earth's growing pains."

This was all incredibly fascinating, and it all resonated in my heart and soul as truth.

Since earliest childhood I'd had a sense that I was somehow much *older* than my physical years. In fact, I remember just before my tenth birthday that I had stopped by the back door into the kitchen and held up both my hands with the fingers apart and marveled that I was *only* going to be ten in earth years when I felt like a million and ten. I used to tell my friends that I felt "a lot older than ten." Also during those early years, and even to this day, I had a weariness that ached deep inside me, and so I often found myself needing a nap when my friends were playing.

My dear Butch used to remark to me constantly when I was sixteen, "You act like you're so old" and "You have to start getting around younger people, because you are more like thirty than sixteen." Ah, beloved Butch. I believe he knew even then. I had to smile at this memory as he, at least in my presence, seemed like he was centuries older than me spiritually. In fact, it was almost incongruous to see him sitting next to me in the form of a teenage boy because something so *ancient and knowing* gazed at me from his warm brown eyes.

I had another question.

"Let's say I wanted to try to access the Akashic Records. How do I learn to do astral projection to get to them?"

She thought for a moment. "Astral projection is simply the soul leaving the body temporarily and being able to travel to other places, times, and dimensions. Sometimes it's called an out-of-body experience and is probably very similar to what you went through with your near-death experiences. Some people have learned techniques so that they can leave their physical body behind easily on command, and others do it through dreaming."

"So it can be learned?"

"Oh, yes. It is easily learned. I've done it many times."

"And have you been allowed access to the records?"

"Only once."

"So how would I learn this technique?"

"I can help you, and there are a few books on the subject you can read and I'll give you the titles." She paused. "You will find that when you are adept at astral projection that your astral or soul self is usually tethered to your physical body by a very strong-looking silver cord that really resembles an umbilical cord. It is said that if this cord is broken or becomes detached in any way, you will die."

Now I began to wonder if I wanted to try out astral projection or not.

Was accessing the records that important to me?

I had a lot to ponder and many decisions to make.

In any event, after this meeting with my mentor, I began to mentally hear a distinct mental *click, click, click* as the puzzle pieces of my life were beginning to fit together in a sensible and true order.

No more than two days after the meeting at the restaurant, I had another incredible dream. Apparently, the opening of my third eye was helping my soul to make rapid advances on its journey to understanding.

In this dream I seemed to be in a place of limitless time and far beyond the realm of Earth, where I drifted along in a vast place I sensed was far, far from my own galaxy. Looking down, I saw that there was an incredibly long silver cord attached to my midsection. This cord vanished down into the clouds and the space behind me, but easily grew and lengthened as I moved upward. I knew it was keeping me attached to my physical body somewhere far below. Suddenly before me the sky seemed to open up, and I found myself in a sort of huge room that seemed to be floating in a void of pure light and cloudless blue sky. All around me massive bookshelves soared upward into the heavens. Everything was in pure white. Even the covers of the books were white.

A very ancient man was seated at a white table. He spoke to me with his mind via a sort of mental-telepathy type of communication that was familiar to me from my many communications with the dead. "What do you seek?" he asked.

"I seek the truth about myself," I replied solemnly with mind talk.

He pointed skyward to the stacks of books.

"There is your record. You may access it briefly by willing it to you."

I looked up at the rows and rows of books and noticed that individual names were printed in gold on the bindings.

Then I saw my book.

I closed my eyes and held out my hands, and the book, neither slim nor fat, drifted slowly onto my open and waiting palms.

I mentally opened the pages and began to read. There in beautifully written script were names and dates and places that had no real meaning to me. Names seemed to be ordered in a fashion that I would later find had a great bearing on my past, present, and future selves. At that point in time, they truly did not resonate with a great deal of my present life, although some names did.

The book began to sort of tingle in my hands, and then it slowly closed and returned to its place on the shelf.

I turned and looked around for the old man, but he was nowhere to be seen.

I looked at the silver cord and began to think about returning to my physical body. There was a feeling of a slight tug downward, and I drifted easily back through the sky and clouds, letting the cord follow my thoughts of return to myself.

I came slowly into my sleeping body and slept peacefully through the night.

The next day at work, I told my friend what I had dreamed. She was considerably shocked. "You have really experienced a lot in a short time. Your learning is more accelerated than anyone else I have ever met. To be allowed admittance to the Akashic Records so soon is absolutely incredible!"

And I did feel that she was correct, yet on another level I took it to be somehow my birthright and not really all that extraordinary—but I did not express this aloud.

I sensed that my soul's path did seem to be accelerating quickly, as if something within me was awakening to a new dawn of possibilities. And I must admit that I wanted to rush forward, now that it was free of the shackles of conventional beliefs.

Again, it was both extremely exciting and very frightening, and I was glad that at least I had one person in my life whom I could talk to and who understood me. I wanted to rush forward into my new life and embrace and learn and grow and return to the me I knew I had once been in centuries past. I wanted to know more about my past self—who and what I had been and done, and after viewing the Akashic Records it was validation that I had lived before because the records were absolute truthful recordings in print.

This reawakening and knowledge seemed as if it had been such a long time in coming, and I felt as if I had trudged through thousands of weary miles to get here at last.

A couple of weeks later I went to the local public library to see if I could find any of the books on reincarnation and the Akashic Records that my mentor had suggested. The offerings were pretty scant, but I did locate some books on the topics.

Over the next few weeks I devoured every book I could, from Edgar Cayce to a children's book about reincarnation. I soaked up every bit of this information like a sponge, absorbing it into my mind and psyche.

I learned some very interesting things, particularly about reincarnation. I learned that while most Americans believe that we live only once, millions of others around the world believe that we are reborn into new lives countless times. There were so many case records that, at least to me, proved the validity of the reincarnation theory. I read the story of Virginia Tighe, a housewife from Pueblo, Colorado, who in 1952 had been hypnotized by businessman Morey Bernstein (hypnotism had been a hobby of Bernstein's for many years).

Regressed to a past life in Ireland, Tighe recounted her life there as Bridey Murphy (1798–1864).

Yet another fascinating case I read about was that of Imad Elawar, a boy from a small village in the mountains of Lebanon. Imad was able to recall a lifetime as a man named Ibrahim Bouhamzy, who had lived and died in a village about twenty miles from where Imad lived. This was another case documented by Dr. Ian Stevenson.

The last case of reincarnation that fascinated me was that of Phil and Ann. They met quite by accident in Malibu, California, when Phil stopped to ask her directions. Their relationship grew close after several meetings, and Phil always had the feeling that they had known one another before and somehow belonged together. Phil had a past-life dream of Ann. He had been a minister named Walter Morris, and Ann had been named Martha Williams. The couple had married and gone to China to work among the poor. The ending of the story was quite tragic, but the truth was validated for Phil when he was actually able to meet the surviving members of the Morris family in the present day and found that events had happened just as he had remembered!

This was so very exciting for me. Oh, I knew that no one could prove scientifically that reincarnation was real—yet something deep inside me was stirring and waking up. I didn't care what science had proven or had been unable to prove. In my heart and soul I *knew* I had lived before—and I had known it since I was an infant.

I also read books about the Buddhist and Hindu beliefs in reincarnation.

My horizons were expanding rapidly.

Now I needed to go to the next step and find out if all the feelings and images that had come to me when I was very young were real.

Not long after this, I was to meet the next person who would bring me to a deeper understanding of my mission and put my feet more firmly on a life path that would challenge me to believe in myself and in my past lives.

Shortly after the dream of the Akashic Records, I decided to see a counselor at a local clinic. I really wanted to explore my own psyche more fully—my issues of abandonment and the unreasonable and absolute terror of childbirth that I'd had since I was very young.

I had no idea that I was about to meet the next teacher on my now-accelerated life path.

It all happened—as I found these synchronistic meetings most often did—in a quick and relatively easy way.

I arrived for my appointment and found that in order to receive counseling I had to fill out paperwork and go over it with an intake worker. After doing the paperwork and a brief wait, I was ushered into an office where a young man in probably his mid-thirties or early forties sat behind a desk. He welcomed me and motioned me to a chair beside the desk and then commenced to explain a questionnaire that he had to fill out with my help.

After we went over my original paperwork together, he began to ask the questions. When he got to the part about my feelings of grief, bereavement, and so forth, I told him about the deaths of my dear grandparents, who had been my real and true parents since I was a newborn. I explained the crushing feelings of loss I experienced when they had died within a few months of one another, and that this grieving for them was still a part of my life well over fifteen years later. Thankfully, the intake session was scheduled for longer than an hour, because after I explained how my grandparents had lovingly raised me and then died when I was eighteen, he sat back and looked at me very closely.

I had the edgy feeling that he was assessing me in much the same way that my mentor at the office had done—but this was more like a probing on a soul level.

Then he asked me if I had ever seen my grandparents' ghosts.

Not even really fazed by his sudden switch of subject matter, I told him without hesitation of the few experiences I'd had with Grandpa's ghost, and the ghosts of several others as well, who had appeared to me in both form and dreams.

He looked off in the distance and then, laying his pen down on the desk, said, "My grandfather also came to me as a ghost right after his death."

From that point on, the conversation no longer had anything to do with me receiving counseling for my original concerns. It drifted off into me talking about my childhood experiences of communicating with the dead, my three near-death experiences, and the recent meeting with my friend at work, as well as my dreams of having received a third eye and being able to access the Akashic Records.

After I shared all of this, a silence fell in the room. Quietly and carefully, he put my paperwork in a file folder, closed it, and put it aside. He leveled a look at me and said words I shall never forget: "No one comes to me by mistake, Marilou."

As with my mentor at the office, I realized that this man was the next person I was meant to meet on my journey to reawakening.

He told me that he was a worker in past-life regression, a method whereby he hypnotized his patients and thus helped them return to their previous lifetimes. He would very much like to see me for an appointment at his office, located several miles away in another county.

He lowered his voice and told me that his work outside the local clinic where we were was not something he publicized, as others would not understand, and, in fact, he could quite possibly lose his job if it were found out that he was a believer in ghosts and reincarnation.

Again, the sense of secrecy surrounding what I thought should be shared joyfully and openly with all was a nearly suffocating blanket thrown over the reawakening in my soul.

The reawakening process was tinged with excitement and that quivery feeling of again standing on the brink of incredible discovery of who I had once been.

The date and time were set, and he gave me directions to his place, which would turn out to be his home/office about a half-hour drive away.

On the way home I pondered deeply the meeting with my new teacher, and I also considered how terrible it was that such things as we had discussed were not spoken of out in the world. I determined that, despite what lay ahead for me, I would not always be afraid to speak aloud what I knew and what I had experienced. I did not believe it was right to try to coerce people into believing as I did—only to write or talk openly about it and give options that might otherwise remain hidden.

Two weeks later I went to my appointment, and it was then that my soul began its amazing backward journey as I was regressed to the first of my past lives.

Chapter Four

THE REGRESSION SESSIONS

Of course I had no idea what to expect on the day I arrived a bit early for my appointment with my newly found past-life regression therapist, and I was both incredibly fearful and amazingly calm.

Both my curiosity and anticipatory levels were very high.

His wife and young sons greeted me at the door when I arrived and brought me to his office, where his wife invited me to sit and relax for a few minutes because her husband was out and would return shortly.

I sat down on a brown leather sofa and looked around the neatly appointed room. The appropriate certificates hung on the walls in frames. There were bookcases and chairs, a desk—the usual office furniture. But for me the best thing of all was the comforting sound of a creek rushing past just outside the wall behind me.

When my therapist finally arrived, he sat down on a chair to my right and we chatted for a few minutes. He shuffled some paperwork as we picked up the thread of the conversation we'd had at his office at the clinic.

Somehow we bypassed the ghostly experiences we had shared, and he focused on my past-life memories.

Again I told him some of the things I had known since I was an infant—things I knew about myself that I had never shared with anyone but Butch. He sat very quietly, occasionally jotting down some notes as I talked. He would often look over at me with intensity and then write some more.

Suddenly he stopped writing, put the pad and pen down on a coffee table between us, and stood up. He went to his desk and returned with a cassette recorder, which he placed on the low table, and then he lit a large, round white candle that had been there next to a box of tissues. He walked over and lowered the lights in the room.

I told him again about the dream I'd had of the beautiful place with the courtyard, the eye opening on the pyramid and in my forehead, and of the priest who had taught me how to use my new eye.

He stopped and looked at me steadily. "That's right. You did tell me that your third eye had opened."

"Yes," I responded.

"Incredible!"

He came back and sat down in the chair to my right and very calmly said, "Marilou, if it's okay I would really like to try a regression session with you today."

For me the moment of truth had arrived.

I felt myself teetering on the brink of discovery just as I had during those long-ago summer days when I had been transported by my swing to other times and places.

But this was radically different from those swinging-back-in-time days—this would take the situation out of my control and put it into the hands of a relative stranger.

I didn't know if I was ready to take such a momentous step.

I didn't give him an answer right away, but sat with my hands folded on my lap while my mind contemplated this turn of events.

Did I *really* want to open this Pandora's box?

My thoughts were a flurry of confused hesitation as caution, curiosity, and excitement battled for dominion in my mind.

Dare I do this—take this step that I had both craved and feared for so long?

Questions assailed me. I gathered them together and put voice to those concerns that were now uppermost in my mind: Would I be hurt by any of this? Would I be put to sleep? How long would it last? Would I remember anything?

And my own inner, unspoken question—could I *really* trust him? After all, I would be allowing him admittance to my deepest memories and most personal fears.

I asked my questions, and he answered each of them calmly and in order and added a little bit of information here and there that eventually put me at ease.

The first point he made was a caution that exactly duplicated what my office mentor had told me—no one but a person certified to perform hypnotism/past-life regression should ever attempt such a treatment on another. He said the reason for this was quite simple: the mind is an incredible thing and very delicate. Many people who had trusted in a friend with a spinning gold watch or some such focal object had gotten to a past life, but they had been unable to get back to the present because the session had been done by an amateur who thought it was all a game. Thus, he said, the patient was lost in another time and lived that event mentally over and over again with life potentially culminating in madness. Of course, most of this sort of thing happened a long time ago when mentalists and hypnotism were a fad—but it could still occur even in our modern times. He stood up and beckoned me to follow him across the room. I did, and he showed me his various certificates and licenses to practice social work and hypnotherapy. They looked quite authentic to me.

We returned to sit down again in our respective places.

He explained that some people were good candidates for past-life regression because they believed in the process and were willing to let go of control. Those who were entrenched in controlling every aspect of their lives and did not want to let go and become part of the process were not such good candidates for a regression.

I told him I didn't know which group I would fall into.

As he spoke I became more at ease, and I felt the all-important trust factor slowly building between us.

Would I be hurt by the experience? He explained that there would quite likely be the *feelings* of pain associated with an accident or illness that I may have had in another time. However, there were means within his repertoire that would alleviate this discomfort for me, such as giving me a command to view the event as if it were a movie and happening to someone else—thus causing me detachment from the agonizing event. This would definitely be invoked if I were to go through a death experience from another lifetime that had been very painful.

He assured me that I would not be put to sleep, but would find myself in a sort of waking dreamtime where I would be fully alert and coherent but at the same time actually feeling as though I were living in my other bodies and times.

He told me that no session with him lasted longer than two hours, simply because it was a somewhat draining experience for anyone to be regressed to another lifetime—especially if that lifetime was full of trauma. He asked me if I had driven there alone or if someone was with me. I told him my husband was outside in the car. He said that this was good due to the mental exhaustion that could result from a regression, causing driving alone for any distance to be difficult, especially at night, which it now was.

And, yes, he said I would remember all of it because he would give me a post-hypnotic command to be able to do that—plus the fact that he recorded all his sessions for his records.

At last I felt calm and sure enough to put my total trust in him.

He turned on the recorder and spoke my name, the date, and the time.

"Now, Marilou. I want you to look at the flame of the candle. Concentrate on it so that it is the only thing you see. The only thing you will hear is the sound of my voice. You will follow my voice and hear me no matter where you are, who you are with, or what you are doing. Do you understand?"

I responded that I understood.

"You may lean back against the sofa or lie down, which-ever you prefer."

I leaned back.

"Please relax your hands on your lap, preferably palms up."

I did as he instructed.

"Now, concentrate on the candle flame and relax. We are going to try to achieve the kind of relaxation that you feel just before you go to sleep. And right now you are getting so very tired that your eyelids are getting heavier and heavier by the second. You very badly want to go to sleep. Soon your eyes will close, and even though you may want to open your eyes and look around, you won't need to. You are safe and comfortable."

His quiet, even tone and inflection were soothing, and I felt very peaceful and actually quite drowsy.

The only sounds were the creek rushing by outside the office, his voice, and the very distant sounds of his sons' voices from another part of the house.

I gave in and let the overwhelming drowsiness encom-pass me as I leaned back against the couch, allowing it to cradle my nearly sleeping form.

The golden glow of the candle flame was all I could see. It seemed to grow larger and larger until my vision was en-compassed with it. My eyes opened and closed a few times and then closed totally, yet somehow the glow of the candle's light remained imprinted on the inside of my eyelids, main-taining a yellow-orange color and radiating a deep feeling of peace and comfort.

I felt myself slide into a deeper state of relaxation, just as I had on the swing when I had mentally let go of my attachment to my body and to Earth time.

It was the oddest sensation, and I can only describe it as feeling as if I were awake and asleep at the same time.

My therapist urged me to breathe deeply and be at peace.

"Now, clear your mind of all the things of the day. There are no more cares. No worries. All is in harmony. No cares. Just peace—the peace of a deep and healing sleep."

I slid deeper into the darkness of sweet oblivion. The voices of my therapist's wife and children faded away until they were like the sound of a television on low volume. I could no longer hear the creek rushing by outside the office window. I seemed to be drifting in a void, but it wasn't scary at all. In fact, it was actually very comforting—a perfect cocoon of peace.

Then he said, "Now. Let's go back to the time you were three years old in this lifetime. Let me know when you are there. When you arrive, tell me where you are, what are you doing, and who is with you."

The scenes of my present life rushed past me almost as if a videotape was being rewound. I saw myself as a twenty-year-old; I saw my grandparents' funerals; then I was eighteen and graduating high school; I was sixteen and deeply in love with Butch, and we were parked on a country road and kissing and drowning in newfound joy. Then I was ten and working in the garden with Grandpa. I was at my ninth birthday party and holding up my most-yearned-for gifts: a plastic bow-and-arrow set and a cap pistol with caps.

My mind shifted as the mists that had obscured the child me parted, and I found myself drifting, drifting until I felt a sort of physical tug as I descended into my past and watched and felt my three-year-old self pick up a fluffy, yellow baby chick and hold it up gently for Grandpa to take. I did not actually drop into my three-year old body but seemed to be a presence standing just behind it and watching the scene play out.

As the baby chick began to peep and its downy, soft feathers tickled my palm, the little girl I had once been turned and smiled at the present-day me standing just behind her! I looked into my own, trusting three-year-old self's eyes and marveled at the fact that we knew one another—she knew my past and knew some of her future. In later years I would find that this type of experience was extremely rare.

I told my therapist what I was seeing and doing and who I was with. As I spoke, my voice sounded as if it were coming from an extremely distant place. It was measured and slow and deliberate as I tried to match the words to the mental image.

"Now, I want you to go back even further, Marilou. All the way back to the time and day of your birth into this lifetime."

I began to tumble, tumble until I felt as if I were sliding down an endless dark passageway. I felt my small body being squeezed painfully, and then the pain released itself and started over again. I could hear distant voices and see a sort of waning yet bright light. I wanted to alternately kick away from and go toward that light and those voices, but each time I tried to go either forward or backward, the horrible squeezing sensation pressed me down.

"Marilou. What is happening to you? If it is stressful, stand back and see it as a movie. Detach from it and tell me what is going on."

I began to speak to him of the sensations I was experiencing. I tried to do as he suggested and to view what was happening to me as if it were a movie, but it didn't work. For a brief moment I felt as if I were somehow split in two and was both fully involved and an observer—almost as if I were in two places at once. I was feeling the painful, overwhelming tug, pull, tug, and squeeze, and then suddenly there was the alarming sensation like something building and opening in my chest and then fading away. There was no air at all, and for the briefest of moments I lingered in some sort of in-between place of both darkness and light—waiting for *something*.

"Relax into the birthing process, Marilou. This is all very natural. It will be over in a little bit."

I heard that distant voice of my therapist speaking to me —grounding me—as my tiny new body fought now to remain both in the soft, familiar darkness I was leaving and also achieve the light I could vaguely see.

There was a final push and tug and voices everywhere. There were murmurings, something metallic, and then I felt the stinging cold air on my warm, wet skin. Hands were on me. I did not dare to open my burning and sensitive eyes to the brightness of the place I was now in. There was a horrible sensation of being held upside down and a sharp, stinging feeling on my backside. There was a rush of fire in my chest, and I began to cry—whimper really—then I escalated into a shrieking cry because of the total indignity I felt.

This whole thing hurt so badly, I recoiled from it with every bit of my tiny being. I wanted to leave the horribleness and return to the peaceful, dark solitude I had known. Oddly, I had the most discomfiting feeling of being totally *alone* while going through this ordeal. There didn't seem to be anyone "on my side." The voice I had remembered from the dark, warm place was silent now. The loss of that closeness that had sustained me was heartbreaking. At this point in time, I had no way of knowing that many women who gave birth in the 1950s were given strong sedatives to help alleviate the pain of childbirth. What it meant for me was that there wasn't anyone familiar to greet me when I arrived back on Earth—my mother was totally absent from my life from the moment I was born.

It was a very lonely feeling.

The entire experience of being born was exhausting, and all I wanted to do was to sleep for a long, long time.

In another portion of my dozing mind, I finally understood why the process of being born or reborn was an experience that was usually wiped clean from the memory slate. The feelings of pain and separation from the comfort of the womb were deeply felt.

But my journey into my distant past wasn't over.

"Okay, Marilou. Good. You've gone back to your birth in this lifetime. Now we need to go even further back. Back to a time before time. Back to the very first time you were ever on Earth in physical form. When you get there, tell me what you see, who you are with, and what you are doing."

I began a rapid free fall into alternating landscapes of light and darkness. A kaleidoscope of swirling confusion occurred as I tumbled backward into my most distant past. Images glided by, and I heard bits of conversation as though a radio were being switched between too many stations too quickly. Garbled noises, sights, and smells assailed my senses: dirt and grass and flowers and cooking aromas all commingled and cleared. It all seemed to go on forever and ever, and I feared that it would never stop.

But stop it did—quite suddenly, as if the brakes on an ancient machine had been slammed on.

And when the swirling mist parted and I felt myself righted, I looked out again at the temples and the white stone walkways and the rising mountains and the beautiful blue sea of the place I knew was Atlantis.

Over the years and when people find out that I am a total believer in reincarnation and that I have been regressed to my past lives, they've asked me what it feels like to undergo a regression. I cannot, of course, speak for others, but I can describe what it felt like for me to have that life-altering experience on several occasions. And if I had to try to give another person the words that would prepare them for the sensations they would feel, I would say that it is like being suspended in that semi-drowsy state just before sleep takes over. The other elements are ones of timelessness and awe, as the vistas of the past lives you have lived open seamlessly for your review.

Then when the actual free fall into the past occurs, it was for me like watching a movie in my mind where I had the lead role. In that movie I was experiencing everything that was going on around me and to me: I felt the sun/rain/snow/wind/whatever weather was occurring at the time. I smelled the scents of the scene I found myself in, be those aromas sweet or rancid. I felt the actual pain of sadness, the joy of love, the anguish of dying, and the relief at leaving behind a sick or injured body and being free to return to that ethereal home some call Heaven or paradise.

Every tiny detail of the life I was in was felt, smelled, heard, seen—every sense was fully engaged.

Make no mistake—a regression session is a journey back to one's most authentic self.

My first session was a joyful and heart-wrenching return to Atlantis.

Sweet Home Atlantis

Oh, dear and most beautiful and beloved Atlantis! What pure joy it was to be back again—even if only in a dreamlike visit during a regression session. All around me the streets once more teemed with the people so well recognized: the children in groups sedately following a priest or adult through the crowded roadways, the market square, the ancient ones—the teachers—moving placidly about among the citizens, the wondrous temples glaring white in the warm and bright sun. Always pervasive and delightful were the intoxicating scents of the exotic plants, and the aromas were so soothing to my reawakening senses.

I stood silently in the square and let the populace move around me. I inhaled deeply the clean, pure flower- and sea-scented air. I listened to an elder give a brief lesson on visualization to a gathering of children, who, like my young boy self, were dressed in pure white robes of the finest gauze-like cloth. I turned, and there were the mighty ships coming into and leaving the harbor—their crews shouting in many different languages as they unloaded their precious cargo. Above the ships was the familiar sight and sound of seagulls squawking and soaring about as they searched hopefully for a bit of food.

I looked up, and above my head smaller pod-shaped aircraft moved with a semi-silent whirring noise. I had not noticed these before but now observed them closely. These air machines had glass bottoms, and I knew that these ships of the air were used to travel around Atlantis. I also knew that on rare occasions they could be used as escape vehicles that could navigate in both the air and in the sea.

My gaze returned to earth level.

It was all so incredibly *real!*

And I felt so incredibly real and comfortable in this young-boy body I inhabited.

Then came the distant and annoying voice tugging at my mind, reminding me that I had an obligation to my future self.

"Marilou! Please answer me! Tell me what you are doing and where you are right now. Is anyone there with you?"

I deeply resented the intrusion but knew I had no choice but to respond. So I began to speak, but this time my voice sounded very different to me. It sounded like me, but it came out of my mouth as the voice of a young boy. It so startled me to hear this unfamiliar tone coming from me that I stopped and started speaking again to see if it would change but it did not, and so I just continued describing what I was seeing.

Dutifully, I told my therapist that I was in Atlantis, and I described for him all of the wonders my eyes were seeing. I admit that it was somewhat difficult to convey the actual reality of the beauty my eyes were viewing or the sensational aromas I was inhaling, but I did my best.

I was about to move around the courtyard when I felt a presence hovering near me and then a light tap on my shoulder.

I *knew* who it was before I even looked up.

The commanding blue-eyed man, or priest, who had been such an integral part of my dreams of Atlantis, the one who had helped open my third eye, was standing beside me.

"Come," he said simply and began to walk with purpose away from me. I followed without hesitation.

A few moments later, we entered the columned doorway of a large and imposing temple. The interior was cool, and a huge fountain bubbled and gushed with water before us. There was a constant tone vibrating through this place as if a large gong were being struck rhythmically. Many other priests walked past and inclined their heads in respect to the man I was following. I kept moving my strong but much shorter legs faster to keep up with him as he seemed to glide-walk through this place.

We came through a doorway into a sort of large, circular open area lit with brilliant sunlight. A kaleidoscope of crystals were upon the walls. There was no roof on this room, and I sensed it was a classroom of some sort. There were white marble steps that encircled one half of the place. There were about thirty or so other children, both boys and girls about my pre-teen age, seated on various levels of the steps. A podium of what looked to be white marble was situated below these semicircular steps that rose up six tiers high. The priest went to the podium and motioned me to take a seat on one of the steps. I climbed to the third-level center and sat down expectantly.

"Today," the priest intoned, looking around at all of us, "we will continue our lesson on levitation. Please focus your attention on me."

Seated next to me was a very beautiful boy who looked to be about my age. He was slim and elegant and had a near-aristocratic bearing. He had the most deep and alluring chocolate brown eyes and wavy, shoulder-length brown hair. He smiled and winked at me, and I had a flash of recognition from my present life, but it was quickly gone. Then we turned our attention back to our teacher, who was now seated cross-legged on the floor beside the podium. His hands rested palms up on his knees, and his eyes were closed.

He seemed very still, and we all collectively held our breath as we waited with anticipation to see what he would do next.

Suddenly, the priest began to rise from the floor and float above it to a height of about two feet above the podium and stayed there.

It was absolutely incredible!

I wondered if I would be able to do that.

As I watched, the priest, who kept his eyes closed during the levitation, drifted slowly back down to the floor. He mumbled something to himself, opened his eyes, and stood up, keeping one hand on the podium as he spoke.

"Now, everyone sit in the position I just did, legs crossed, palms facing upward. Close your eyes and concentrate on what you want your body to do. The body must always follow the dictates of the mind, and it will do as you will it to if you believe and allow the power to flow through you."

Before I did as the priest instructed, I took a moment to glance around me. Everyone was sitting cross-legged with their palms facing upward.

I did the same, and even though I knew I was at a disadvantage because I had not had the previous lessons my classmates had, I still believed I could achieve this skill.

An overwhelming hum of expectation seemed to energize the room.

I closed my eyes and visualized myself able to float above the step I was seated on.

At first I had the feeling that it wouldn't work at all. My body felt heavy and unresponsive, and I was very disappointed. I wanted so badly to prove myself.

I concentrated more deeply, moving mentally away from the stimuli going on around me—the cries of birds above and the shuffling of the other children as they sought a comfortable position.

Then I felt it—the slightest of tingles through my body like a sort of delicate electricity that was in no way unpleasant. I began to feel as if I were lighter than air; in fact, I had been visualizing that I was as light as a feather. I kept concentrating, and suddenly I no longer felt the cold stone beneath me but rather air moving past. I wanted to open my eyes but didn't dare do so for a few moments.

Then curiosity got the better of me, and I opened them a bit and looked down.

I was actually floating about a foot above the step!

What an exhilarating feeling!

The boy next to me was only a few inches above his seat, and several of the others—girls mostly—were having some difficulty with levitating and staying up when they did manage it. They kept going up and down or drifted a few inches left or right, went down, and came back up again.

Most of the other children now had their eyes open as well, and we were observing one another.

Meanwhile, I was totally enjoying my newfound skill, and the priest was pointing me out to everyone as the best in the class.

I had never had any sensation like that, yet on some level I realized that it was very much like the feeling of no longer being earthbound that I had experienced as a three-year-old on my swing. It flashed quickly through my mind that when I had been on my swing in my future lifetime that I probably had been trying to re-create these levitation skills.

"All right, everyone. Time to return, to come back down and get ready for the next lesson and visualization."

I drifted easily back down and felt the solid cold stone beneath me. I looked over at my new friend, and he smiled at me as he too settled again on the stone seat.

"Good. Very good," the priest said, glancing at all of us proudly. "Now, everyone get together with a partner for the next lesson, and we will go outside."

As if in unison, the slim boy and I looked at one another, and without a word passing between us, we got up together and walked outside with the others.

We sat down on a grassy area just outside the temple. Through the trees I could see the waves rolling up onto the shore. It was so beautiful out here!

"This will be a lesson in telepathy. Decide between you which one of you will be the sender and which one the receiver," the priest said as he walked among us. "What I want the sender to do is to think of anything you wish—perhaps a simple object familiar to all. Hold that image in your mind and then try to send that image mentally to your partner."

My friend and I looked at one another. He nodded at me, and I knew I was to be the sender. We closed our eyes. I immediately saw the image of a seagull come into my mind. I held it there.

"When you have the image firmly in your mind, send it to your partner."

I waited for a few moments until I had every detail of the gull imprinted in my mind, and then I sort of mentally pushed the image to my friend.

"When the receiver has the image, raise your hand."

We were each picked in turn. Many had gotten their images just right.

Of course my partner had done perfectly. As he said, "Gull" in his soft voice, I was filled with joy that he had gotten it right.

At this point I seemed to sort of leave the lawn behind and drift in a gray, misty place of no sound. Of course, the whole time I was going through the lessons on levitation and telepathy, I had been informing my therapist of what was occurring.

The mist cleared at last, and I found I was walking along the seashore of Atlantis with the priest. I had no idea how much time had passed since the telepathy lesson, but it seemed like only a few days. The priest was talking to me about my "third eye" and telling me that it would soon be time for me to have it open on a more consistent basis. He called it my "soul eye" and explained that it would open doors for me to other realms that were beyond my imagination. I listened to everything he said, doing my best to recall his words and his presence with me. I was very proud to be walking alone with him and felt that I had somehow been singled out for some special reason. I experienced intense gratefulness for this time with him in this beautiful place.

It was odd to consider, but I found that I did know my name and my teacher's name but could not pronounce them. When the therapist asked me during the session for names, I could only report that my teacher's name began with the letter *A*, and that my name began with an *S*.

My teacher and I strolled along several shadowy and sun-lit, sandy paths, keeping our quiet counsel. We were together in our solitude, and words between us eventually became unnecessary. All paths led back into the city. At several points along the way, he began to tell me about the various temples. The one I was most interested in was known as the Healing Temple, and it was a huge edifice that glowed with a radiance that pulsated with a soothing energy. We stopped before it, and I watched as many of the citizens of Atlantis went in and came out.

"There is no disease here," my teacher said as he nodded occasionally to passersby. "If there is a disturbance in the body, it is easily readjusted by unblocking the energy centers of the body—the chakras—with the use of various crystals. Do you remember what the energy centers are?"

In real time I had no knowledge of this subject, yet as a twelve-year-old boy and a citizen of Atlantis, I rattled them off as easily as if I was reciting the alphabet. "Root, sacral, solar plexus, heart, throat, third eye, crown."

"That is correct," the priest said.

We walked closer to the Healing Temple but did not go in.

There was a question burning in my mind and I had to ask it, as I feared I may not have the chance again.

"What about death? Do we ever die here?"

My teacher looked off into the distance and seemed to weigh his words carefully. "There is death, but it is a choice, not a necessity. Sometimes people get tired and want a long sleep, so they go to a particular chamber in one of the temples and are encapsulated in a crystal vault and their essence is absorbed. Their soul returns to life in a new body when it is their time. They reincarnate."

"Oh," I said. "Death is a choice."

"It is."

I looked at his kindly yet ancient body. "Have you ever died?"

"No, I have not. I have been alive in this lifetime for many hundreds of years."

"Aren't you tired?" I asked with the naiveté of a young boy.

"No. But one day if I become tired, I will gladly seek death and a long rest before rebirth."

I watched as a ship sailed past, followed by a flock of gulls.

I wanted to ask more about the crystals and chakras, but the voice of my therapist was echoing too loudly in my mind—pulling me back to the present and to the real me that existed thousands of years in the future.

It was with great reluctance that I followed the voice and left my teacher behind on the shores of that most beloved land.

Waking up and coming to reality in the present was not at all easy. I was very groggy and disoriented and still clung mentally to the incredible joy I had experienced at being back in Atlantis.

When I was more fully awake, my therapist and I had a long discussion about Atlantis and especially my teacher there. My therapist was very interested in the physical description of the man, and I again told him—mentioning the most singular and outstanding feature being the piercing blue eyes. That spiraled our conversation to my own personal meetings with my guardian angel, who had appeared to me on three occasions in my life: twice to bring healing and the third time after a near-fatal car accident when he came to take me to Heaven or Paradise to allow me to see there all of my relatives, friends, and pets who had passed over.

As we talked, I began to realize the similarities between my Atlantean priest and the guardian angel—the most telling one being again that of the incredible blue eyes. The eyes of both men were alight with a fire that seemed to burn from somewhere deep within and to shine with great knowledge, love, and compassion that was achingly beautiful. I did not think that these two were related in any way or that they might be gods, as my therapist suggested. I had the distinct impression that they were godlike, in that all of my youthful Christian upbringing had taught me of the kindness and wisdom of the being I knew as Jesus. No, I saw these two as totally separate yet cut from the same cloth of unconditional purity and love. They resonated with an *ancientness* that echoed through time and through my soul and touched something very deep inside. The comfort each one brought was a touchstone that I needed to make me feel connected to the place and places I called home. I had experienced this sensation of resonance only a couple of times in my life by the time of these sessions: with my first true love, Butch, whose soul melded with mine at our very first meeting; and with the man who was, at that time, my husband—the one I had dreamt of when I was sixteen.

Of course, I had shared with my therapist the dreams I'd had at age sixteen, the most telling of which was my death by drowning during the cataclysm that engulfed and destroyed that beautiful city of Atlantis. I now knew that the man in the boat with the unforgettable blue eyes and the signet ring had been my priest there, and he had done his best to save me but to no avail.

It must be remarked that at this point in my life I had yet to re-meet my Atlantean teacher, and like my present spouse, my co-workers, my therapist, Butch, and the others I knew, his return to my life would happen when it was time. And when it happened a few years in the future, it would be in a very interesting way.

On the ride home that night, I couldn't help but contemplate the absolute wonder and privilege I had known being a citizen of that most incredible of civilizations. The skills I had developed that lay dormant within me were mind-boggling. That singular lifetime had been the basis for all that was to come—a firm foundation upon which to build my dreams of writing and being able to share my experiences with the world.

I was starting to truly understand my own soul's journey and its real purpose here on Earth.

I was eagerly looking forward to my next regression session.

A Celtic Lifetime

This lifetime seemed, oddly enough, to be a natural progression from the Atlantean one, mainly because it was in such opposition to the peaceful and serene prior tine spent in Atlantis.

Further, I had the sense that centuries had passed since my last incarnation.

This regression session would throw me immediately into the midst of quite a horrible bit of action, as I found my life at stake as well as the life of another very familiar person.

As I settled into my spot on the sofa in my therapist's office and he gave me the now-familiar instructions, I was almost quivering with anticipation.

Where would I end up?

Would I find happiness or sadness?

These regression sessions were, to me, like reading a mystery book of my own life and, just like reading that page-turner, I wanted to read all the chapters at once.

I fell very quickly into this lifetime with no knowledge of my life circumstances. My first impression upon arrival was of green everywhere: green leaves, emerald-green grass, and green moss embellishing huge rocks. The next sensation was of warmth and the wet-blanket feeling of a humid summer day with the sun either just rising or setting. It seemed as though it had recently rained, as there was a clean, fresh rain-shower scent in the air and dampness all around me.

Yet every one of these images and scents and sensations were fleeting as I felt my heart pumping furiously in my chest as I ran in terror through fields and forests, leaping over roots and rocks and trying desperately to stay on my feet because stumbling and falling would mean certain death. Even though my panic was great, the images filled my mind with indescribable vividness and intense clarity.

I must have been breathing heavily or giving some indication to my therapist that I was in distress, for his voice came to me from a great distance. "Marilou! Try to remain calm. If you would like, observe this as a movie scene. Let me know what's happening."

I had no time to communicate with someone I knew to be light years away from what was happening to me now. I was fully involved in staying alive and could barely breathe, much less talk. I could not gather my thoughts into any cohesive pattern enough to simply envision this horror-ridden race for life as a mere movie.

It was just too *real*.

I was running in terror. Some things became known to me as I catapulted toward some unknown safety. I knew that I was female, probably between sixteen to eighteen years of age, and slim, with long, wavy dark hair. I was being chased by a group of men who wore long robes, but I could not tell the color of the robes because those I sensed to be men remained as shadow figures that seemed to eat up the daylight as they came steadily after me. I glanced back once and quickly, and they appeared to glide forward effortlessly over the rock-strewn terrain, intent as any group of predators certain of their prey and not too concerned about it escaping.

As I ran, another thought streaked though my mind—I knew I was in the British Isles and these ones chasing me were holy men, Druids, the learned priests who practiced human sacrifice.

And if they caught me, I would to be the next to die.

My errant thoughts and loss of concentration on my running caused me to trip and fall on a tree root, and they were upon me.

I was grabbed roughly and carried at a quick pace back along the way we had come. I struggled to no avail and finally went limp, feigning acceptance of my fate. Beneath my outwardly calm exterior, my mind was racing with plans of escape from what I knew was coming—the sacrifice of my body in a ritual to appease a god.

The next memory I had was of being in a grove of enormous oak trees. I had been put down and was standing with a guard of the robed men around me while another group of robed figures conversed in an unfamiliar tongue. A bonfire had been lit a short distance away and the flames leapt high, crackling and sparking into the day-lit sky. The flames seemed as hungry for my death as those gathered around me. Directly in front of me was a large, almost black stone slab with many strange carvings along the edge and atop it that I could not make out. There was also something else that made my stomach churn—the coppery smell of fresh blood assailing my nostrils.

Something or someone had been killed here and not too long ago.

I felt sick and dizzy, as if I were about to faint.

But wait!

Another man was being pushed forward roughly into the grove and forced to lie on the stone slab, which I knew was an altar. Several of the robed ones held him fast and tied his hands and legs with leather straps that were hooked through iron rings at each corner of the slab. I observed the young man closely. He was tall with reddish-brown hair and deep blue eyes. He seemed to be about twenty years old. He looked across at me imploringly.

A chill coursed through me.

I knew those eyes! They were the eyes I had promised myself I would never forget—the very same ones I had seen smiling down at me in another time and place when I had been the student and he had been my teacher. The same eyes that had looked down at me in pity when I slid for the last time beneath the waves of a dying civilization.

Despite his younger appearance, I knew this was my Atlantean priest!

The men in the grove were now talking excitedly among themselves and glancing at my priest and me. I could not understand their words, but it seemed to me that they were very pleased with having both this man and myself as sacrifices.

The next few minutes were filled with the young man and I trying to make eye contact and finding that, miracle of miracles, we were able to manage to communicate telepathically!

He told me with his mind that he remembered me.

I returned the message that I knew him also.

He said telepathically, "Watch for the way to be clear very soon. Make your move then and free us."

I acknowledged that I would.

Just then another hooded figure entered the grove. There was something very imposing and very frightening about this singular man. Something in his bearing was more regal than the others, and he emanated a powerful aura. He moved to the altar. From somewhere in the folds of his robe he removed a large and horrible-looking knife. He was uttering some words as he stood above the young man. He had the knife clutched in both hands. All the other figures present were murmuring some sort of chant that built into a low crescendo—like a humming of encouragement.

Suddenly, I knew what I had to do.

Taking advantage of their distraction, I burst from between my guards and rushed at the man with the knife. Using all my strength, I knocked him sideways. He fell hard and the knife glanced off the side of the altar, just missing the young man. The knife clattered to the rocky ground at my feet. I quickly picked it up, feeling its deadly cold weight in my hands. I backed against the altar. Strangely, the men did not approach me but hovered at the outer rim watching me closely. The fallen man stayed put, looking up at me with steely gray eyes full of both awe and hatred.

Something about the knife was keeping them all at bay.

I quickly reached behind me and felt for the strap binding the man's left wrist to the altar. I looked quickly, making sure that I would not cut my teacher's skin, and then sawed through the binding. The knife cut easily through, and that got one of his hands free. While he undid himself, I kept the knife out in front of me. No one approached us at all—indeed, they seemed to be in shock and in awe of my unaccustomed bravery.

The young man was loose. I mentally told him to run.

He was concerned about my safety.

I told him to get away, and I would find him when the time was right.

In the midst of this, my therapist's voice hammered in my mind anxiously, seeking to communicate with me. I spoke aloud, "I'm okay." And that silenced him for a moment.

I remember glancing to my right and watching my teacher rush off through the trees and rocks until he was out of sight.

Something told me that he would find safety.

I moved slowly toward the direction he had gone. The men moved forward a pace. The fallen one stood up and watched me intently. I could see no facial features, but I knew he was ready to pounce.

Keeping the knife firmly clenched in my hand, I turned and ran through the trees and again leapt over roots and rocks following the path my teacher had taken.

And that was all.

I do not know what happened to me that lifetime, as I had no image of any further experiences or of my death. Even though, on my return to my present life, my therapist tried to get me to a death scene, there was none to be found. It was as if I simply ran off that day into the forest and vanished from the face of the earth.

Moreover, I had no memory of meeting up again in that lifetime with the young man, my dear Atlantean priest, whose life I had saved.

When I came out of the session and was fully in the present moment, my therapist said he thought, as I had, that this lifetime was one I had lived in the British Isles and that most likely the young man and I were definitely to have been sacrificed by Druids, who were indeed the priests, scholars, physicians, poets, and lawyer types who were manifest throughout the British Isles and France spanning a period in history from the second century BC to the fourth century AD. I'd had no inkling of their existence up until that point, and I wasn't really too interested in learning anything further about them, as they seemed to me—as the priests, lawgivers, and so forth of their time—to be hypocritical in their dealings with their fellow humans.

At home later that night, I had an interesting thought—my favorite tree since age three had always been the oak, and indeed this was the tree I had climbed when I was that age and trying to reach the sky and be taken back home. It was the tree my grandpa and I had always sat under after a long day of berry-picking in the fields and forests behind Pleasant View. It had been the tree my childhood best friend and I had stood beneath when we had pricked our fingers with a briar to become blood sisters.

Perhaps that was coincidence—perhaps not.

EGYPT

One of the truest tests of having an inkling that one has lived in another time and place is an overwhelming attachment or incredible draw to that place and time in history—and I definitely had that attraction to ancient Egypt.

When I was young, I had been fascinated, to a nearly obsessive level, by ancient Egypt. I had no idea then, of course, why I was so *drawn* to that culture, but I had constantly, during those days, borrowed repeatedly the same books from the library on the history of the place. I never grew tired of reading the same paragraphs over and over again or looking at the photos of pyramids and hieroglyphics. In fact, that amazing written record of the history and the people seemed so *familiar* to me, and I felt that with a little training I would again be able to read it easily.

By the time I was in sixth grade, I announced to my grandparents and all my friends that I wanted to be an archeologist as well as a writer when I grew up, so keen was I to somehow find a way to return to that most desired of civilizations—a place I knew had been a part of my life somehow.

At singular intervals I also felt a near repulsion for the time and the place—as if amidst the brightness of the days a dark shadow hovered over something there for me that was very personal. Unaware even of the truth of the term *reincarnation* during my life up until I met my mentor at the office in the 1980s, I had no label for these feelings but continued in my later college days to read as much on the times as I could. My interest waned as I entered my early twenties and then faded altogether as life led me to marriage and employment. The vague dream of becoming an archeologist went out of my mind, as if it had been a candle that had been blown out by an errant wind.

In any event, the reasons I felt as a young girl for wanting to return to the Egyptian culture had to do with an intense *draw* that I felt somewhere deep inside me. It was no mere whim but an attachment I had to the place that defied explanation. Certainly no one I knew had ever traveled there, nor had I. Yet I knew that landscape was oh-so-very familiar to me for some unknown reason. It was another place that felt like *home*, and I yearned for it as much as I had yearned for those mysterious beings of my three-year-old days—the ones I knew could take me back with them and away from the turmoil of earthly life.

So, again the stage was set for this next regression session.

Now familiar with the process and feeling no anxiety even after the last terror-filled Celtic lifetime, I sat calmly on the couch in my therapist's office. The candle was lit; the tape recorder turned on; the lights dimmed. I leaned back and put my hands on my lap with palms up, and he began with the usual instructions about feeling sleepy. I again felt the drifting sensation as I closed my eyes and let the sound of his voice lead me as the attachment to the present loosened its hold.

"Marilou, I'd like you to move to another lifetime that meant a great deal to you. The last time you were in the British Isles. Now move forward in time to the next of your earthly lives. When you get there, tell me what you see and who is with you."

I relaxed deeply again, allowing the candle's flickering flame to encompass both my outer and inner vision. The twilight sleep overtook me, and I fell into it as one does a familiar warm and cozy blanket on a cold winter's night. This time the transition to my distant past was smoother with no tumbling, out-of-control sensations or darkness and distress. It seemed as if I simply awoke in another place.

The first thing I felt was the intense heat of the sun on my head.

I looked around me and found that I was standing under the roof of a huge, temple-like building very reminiscent of my Atlantean days. I moved back farther into the cooler shadows and stood next to a huge column. Instinctively, I recognized the fact that I was a girl between the ages of fourteen to sixteen. As in Atlantis, my attire was a sort of gauzy white dress and on my feet were sandals. I was again tall and slim. I reached up to touch my hair and found that it was shoulder-length and done in many tiny braids. Pulling one of the braids around so that I could look at it, I saw that my hair was very dark.

"Do you know what time period in history you are in?" asked my therapist.

I told him without hesitation that I was living during the reign of the Great Pharaoh Ramses the Second.

"Do you know your name?"

At first my name came to me as starting with the letter *M* and then as the letter *I* and had to do with being named after a goddess.

"Are you a daughter of Ramses?"

This I felt was possible, but I did not know.

I did sense that I was of a very wealthy class of people yet I did not feel so. I mostly felt lonely and lost for some reason—as if a very important piece of the puzzle of my life was missing.

As I stood gazing out across the hot, sandy expanse in front of me, several people who I knew were servants to my family moved past and inclined their heads to me.

I smiled at them wanly.

The deep sense of loneliness and displacement was a harsh burden on my heart, and I was without knowledge of its source.

I lifted my eyes and shielded them from the sun as I looked across a great expanse of land.

In the distance an amazing thing was happening—a gigantic stonework monument was being built. There were hundreds of dark-skinned men moving about the forming base. Most incredible of all was that I could see no visible support system or any stockpiles of massive stone, tools, or equipment of any kind. There was a system of scaffolding made from what I supposed were tree trunks that encircled the side of the structure. The workmen were milling about the thing in droves, moving from one side to the other. This one side I was seeing appeared to be about the height of a two-story house.

I only wondered briefly about how the structure was being raised before a thought hit me like a sledgehammer—*he wasn't here!*

The man I so desired to have in my life was not, I knew, in the throng of men around the pyramid nor was he, I sensed, anywhere at all in this time period!

My heart sank like a stone, and I felt a wash of deep sorrow and loneliness throughout every part of me.

A sensation of abandonment cascaded through me like a dull blade that slowly, inexplicably worked at my psyche as I began to feel separated from my self—my soul and body seeming to come apart and exist at an extreme distance from one another.

Where was he?

Who was he?

A whispering voice came into my mind: "He is the priest—your teacher from Atlantis. He is the one you seek. He didn't get a chance to return this lifetime. You came back too soon."

I felt unsteady on my feet and grabbed the side of the column for support.

That was it!

Something had gone horribly wrong, and I was totally and horribly alone!

I let the thought sink in and then straightened myself and stood without support.

I knew on the deepest level of my being that there was no reason for me to live any longer. It wasn't a scary thought at all. It was just a knowing that I had to acknowledge.

There was no fear or remorse attached to this—I knew that in order to find this beloved man and be reunited with him that I must die, and I knew that my mind was the means by which I could shut down my body and allow it to leave the Earth plane.

I have no recollection of becoming ill, but the next thing I knew I was lying on a bed with many servants rushing about. One was fanning me. Faces peered down at me in grave concern—faces of those I recognized as my beloved father, mother, sisters, and brothers. One brother in particular seemed oddly familiar to me. Tall, slim, with compassionate brown eyes—he looked so like my friend from the Atlantean temple where I had learned to levitate that it was almost enough to make me want to come back and talk to him.

We gazed at one another knowingly, and then he faded from my sight as he moved away from my bed.

I felt so very tired and weak. I just wanted to go from here and be free of this body and this lifetime. I wanted to go and find my love, my teacher, the man who had taught me so much.

In communication with my therapist, he realized that I was about to go through the death experience. His voice came clearly and soothingly. "Stay calm now, Marilou. I want you to observe what is happening as if it on a movie screen. You may, as you already know, go through a few sensations of release but nothing you cannot handle."

The awareness of drifting came to me, and as I watched it as an observer, it was as if I were physically present as both my past life and present self while maintaining different angles of vision. I moved my vision and a sort of astral self about the bedchamber. At first I stood near the foot of the bed, then to the side, then I floated above my form, looking down at it with detachment yet great love and empathy.

The pale, slim, and beautiful body I had inhabited so briefly looked familiar yet foreign to me. As I watched the small chest rise and fall, I was overcome with an incredible sense of panic for a few moments, and on the sofa—my therapist later told me—my own breathing increased to a panting level. The familiar voice of my therapist invaded my mind. "Easy now, Marilou. The transition is beginning. Maintain your distance and let it happen."

I calmed a bit but still had a brief and incredible desire to stop the process. I almost wanted to will my wasted self to rise up and live and eat some of the food that had been offered to me.

Beside my bed my parents hovered with anxious dark eyes. My mother was clasping her hands together and crying.

I wanted to reach up to her to give her strength, but I was too tired and the darkness was pulling me under. I knew that surrendering to the darkness would bring the light and then the peace and freedom I craved to get on to the next life.

So, with a last blurred look at my parents, I released my life.

I heard the sounds of the world fade as I sank deeper and deeper into the sweet oblivion I had craved.

At the end of the darkness was the light I had waited for, and there standing so calmly and quietly, his eyes full of love and understanding, was my Atlantean priest!

He held out his hand to me, and I ran forward and took it.

I was overcome with joy that he had been the one waiting for me!

I wanted to look back at my body, but I did not.

That body and that lifetime no longer mattered as much to me as what lay ahead.

⁓

After I awakened from this regression session, I was very thirsty and was given water to drink. I was shaky and disoriented, as it seemed I had lived through a whole series of simultaneous lives and events: tethered to the present day, dying in another time, experiencing my own longed-for death in that time, and then my transition to the other side and into the comforting presence of the priest.

I also felt an all-encompassing exhaustion that made me want to just lie down on the sofa and sleep for hours.

But, of course, I could not.

About a half hour or so later, I finally got enough of my strength back to stand up and go out to the car, where thankfully my husband had been waiting for me.

On the way home I fell into a deep sleep and did not wake up until we pulled into the driveway.

The next day at work, I told my mentor about this newest experience. She listened intently to my story and did not seem fazed at all about the death event—in fact, she nodded her head several times as I spoke and later acknowledged that she understood everything I had gone through.

Then she told me some news that devastated me for a few days.

She would be leaving soon to work and live elsewhere. She had family in various western and Midwestern states and other work she felt she needed to be doing.

She handed in her resignation letter shortly after this, and on her next-to-last day at our workplace, she and I went out to lunch at the restaurant we had gone to when she had given me the first talk.

I will never forget her response to me when I asked for her new address or a way to get in touch with her again if I needed her: "I have no idea where I will eventually end up, Marilou. And it could be that you and I will never again connect in this lifetime—at least in physical form. But make no mistake: we are all connected on the great web of life, and when we need one another we merely have to send out a telepathic message and the other will hear it and respond if need be. This will also happen when either one of us leaves the Earth plane and transitions to spirit—the surviving friend will sense the absence of the other on a soul level."

This was not at all what I wanted to hear!

She must have seen the fear on my face as she finished speaking. Laying her hand atop mine across the table, she said, "Don't worry. We have touched spiritually in this lifetime, and most likely we have been together in a past life and will meet again. I'll never be any further away than a thought."

I started to protest. "But—"

She interrupted, removing her hand from mine. "You've already found out that those that die return in spirit to visit you in form and dreams. You've had regression sessions and found out that even though you have died that you return to be with the same loved ones again. It is all a cycle. It is never-ending until all the lessons are learned." She paused. "All relationships have a beginning, a middle, and an ending. Children grow up and move away from home. Marriages and love relationships begin and end. Why? Simply because the lessons those souls needed to learn together are over. It is time to move on to the next. There is no sin in accepting the ending of anything. Yes, it is sad. But it also brought home to me that old adage about a door closing and a window opening up. You already sensed this at a very early age. And now further proof is being given to you because this new teacher—this therapist—has come into your life."

Sadly, I knew what she was saying was true.

"And I am leaving because my time in your life is over. You have your new mentor. His arrival in your life signaled my time to leave. After him will come someone else and after that another someone. They will all be teachers to help you on your life journey. Granted, some of them may be as nasty as can be. But you can learn many lessons from the nasty ones as well. Lessons about tolerance, empathy, sympathy, compassion, and most of all—forgiveness."

I did consider that even at this stage of my life I had certainly already met my fair share of the nasty types, but in an odd way, each one I met who treated me badly and whom I forgave and moved on from, gave me experience for the next.

The next day was Friday, and she left for her new life.

I went to work on Monday morning and wandered down the hall to the office my mentor had once occupied. All was very quiet, and the room had that almost tomb-like feeling of darkness and endings. A few posters were still on the walls; the desk had a pencil and pen holder and a calendar mat. But the essence was gone already. I had this feeling come over me that my mentor had probably been right—we would never again meet in this lifetime—but I wouldn't give up hope.

A BENEDICTINE MONK

Although a bit of a surprise to me, thankfully this next lifetime was one of peace and contentment—almost as if a beneficent universe was granting me a reprieve from the tragic endings I had undergone in my previous lifetimes. Again, I had no knowledge of how much time had passed since I had been in physical form, but I sensed it might have been centuries.

I also divined that I was again in the British Isles.

Once more I was a male. I guessed my age to be about twenty years, yet as I found myself seated at a wooden table in brown monk's attire, I felt so much older than my actual physical years.

The centuries weighed upon me, and I felt a great spiritual tiredness within my slim form, but I had no knowledge of my past lives on any level—I only knew that I was, for the most part, content and at peace with my life.

I had entered this lifetime tentatively. I don't recall any transition—no falling, gliding, spinning through a kaleidoscope of images.

It was odd and somewhat difficult to describe, but it was as if I came into the room where I sat as a monk, observed myself from a distance, and then became one with my man self. It was very reminiscent of the time I had first been regressed to my three-year-old self and had not actually been me but observed me holding the baby chick up for Grandpa.

I had entered my monk's body just as we both sighed with contentment.

It was very easy also to maintain contact with my therapist, telling him in detail what I was seeing and feeling.

This lifetime was one of taking joy in simple things and doing tasks that were uncomplicated and routine. I was a scribe, and I copied text onto beautiful paper that felt to my fingers like parchment. I dipped my feathered pen into a bottle full of black ink and wrote and dreamed. Sometimes I even used a tiny amount of the ink I was allotted to write little stories and poems on scraps of old paper. These poems were mostly about the beauty of my surroundings and my love of God. I knew that I secreted them away under a floorboard beneath my bed.

Often I would look out the window of my very tiny and uncluttered room. The scene outside was alluring enough that I often sat quietly contemplating the verdant green fields, the soaring clouds—the sound of birdsong permeating my senses with a delight that thrilled me. A part of me longed—no, yearned—to be free. Another part was quite content to be in the embrace of such holiness and simplicity. It was no matter, this yearning to run once again through the hills and valleys I had delighted in as a young boy, for these urges could no longer be fulfilled. I had left those days far behind—as far behind as I had left the hope of physical love. Here in the monastery I knew that freedom to leave the confines of the place was only granted by someone known as an abbot. I further knew that I was most fortunate to have been accepted into the order a few years in the past. I knew I had experienced severe loss in my youth—that my parents were dead—and that I had come here to find refuge from loneliness and poverty.

There was a severe sense of abandonment existing in my soul, and it hearkened back to that previous lifetime I had lived when I had willed myself to die so young because I felt alone and lost without my priest. And even though in this lifetime I had no knowledge of my Egyptian lifetime, nevertheless it echoed in my soul as a vast emptiness, unnamed and unpleasant. Truthfully, I acknowledged to myself as I sat there that I had no real or compelling desire for relationships of any sort—except my one with God. God had come to mean solace to me—an all-knowing and caring father figure, and in my inventiveness of mind I called upon his presence during prayer time each day. I sought his strength and his unconditional love as a cat does a warm saucer of milk on a cold winter's day. In the embrace of my Lord I was serene.

One day blended into the next in an easy way. There were chores laid out for all of us in the Order. I had alternately tilled the soil, planted gardens, and helped with the sick and destitute who came for help or who were brought to our doors. I found that being of service to others was something that soothed my soul and gave me great joy. I had performed all the required menial tasks given to me: washing, cooking, cleaning. I had helped bury our dead in a little cemetery space behind the monastery. We lived our lives out here and died in the hope and joy of reuniting with God in Heaven.

I knew that I was not allowed to travel away from the monastery, but that didn't mean I didn't yearn for an occasional foray into the villages nearby just to experience seeing other people and how they lived.

But I suffered no ill effects from my solitude and was at peace with myself and my vows.

I was deeply contemplating my beautiful life and reveling in the solitude around me when my therapist's voice called across time to me. "Marilou, where are you and what are you doing? Is anyone there with you?"

I found that I had developed the habit of taking leave quickly of the present during these later regression sessions and going deeply within the soul of my past selves without keeping in constant contact with my therapist. It seemed such an intrusion to have to be in verbal communication with him, as it detracted from my absolute involvement in the time I was living. The sessions were now becoming a release from other present-day issues I was finding it hard to face.

For one, my marriage was dissolving—and the need to say goodbye was understood but it was also taking a toll on me. I had taken on the care of my niece and nephew, and that had brought about friction at work and my supervisors were haranguing me about making the choice of caring for the children or keeping my job—they wanted me to make a choice between having employment and keeping the children. It was a choice I could not make, and so I went to work every day fearing what was going to happen. The sessions with my bosses were often ending with me in tears and feeling pulled in all directions.

As for my marriage ending, I knew that it was the right time. We had both completed our interrupted journey together, and I had no regrets. I had the courage to go forward alone, if need be, realizing that my past lives and my present life had taught me about letting go with love and understanding of the cyclic nature of all things.

Still, it was also heartbreaking and difficult to face an uncertain future and to become a single foster parent working at a job that had so many days tinged with harassment and unkindness.

Thus it was that the regression sessions were now my escape and my solace.

To my therapist I reluctantly and ponderously answered, my voice rumbling deep in my chest—a man's voice—young and full of spirit and light yet also reverent and devout of purpose. I spoke of what I was doing and seeing and that I was alone.

"Do you know your name?"

"Stephen," I answered quietly and without hesitation.

As Stephen I again took up my task of penning the text of the manuscript that was before me.

I was totally at peace and content with this time period.

"Okay," my therapist said, interrupting my writing flow, "let's move forward a bit in this lifetime. When you get there, tell me where you are and if anyone is with you."

I seemed to fall into some sort of dreamy trance while seated at my wooden desk. I closed my eyes and had the sensation of having a dream within a dream.

I now found myself in a room with several hand-hewn tables and benches. It was the evening meal time. I ate my stew quietly and looked around me at the others who were a part of the Order. Some were very young—about ages twelve to seventeen. There were men of my age group, and then it seemed there was a gap in generations until there were the ones just becoming gray-haired. The abbot was a rather rotund man who I knew was the epitome of holiness, fairness, and compassion. I emulated this man as he seemed to possess many of the qualities I was presently lacking. I was often too impetuous, too forward, and too stringent with my words. These qualities were something I knew I had to work on, and this was the most beneficent of atmospheres for me to reside in to temper these few restless frustrations.

I described all of this to my therapist, listening to myself talk in my slow and precise male voice. I actually felt the words forming somewhere deep inside me—as if communicating with words was a hardship or an unused skill I didn't need very much as a monk.

"Now, we are going forward in this lifetime to its end. Let me know when you get there."

I seemed to be yanked from my meal and swept through a tunnel of darkness and light. I was buffeted by unseen winds until I came to the final scene of my peaceful life as a monk named Stephen.

I was in my room, lying on my cot. I could vaguely see the first light of dawn coming in through the small window. It was winter. I was weak and so tired. I craved the oblivion of the long sleep that would reunite me with my Lord and God. I could hear movement beside me and knew that a few of the other monks were praying quietly. I did not know how old I was but sensed it could not have been more than twenty years since I had sat at my desk copying manuscripts and gazing longingly out the window to the fields beyond.

"What is happening? Are you getting ready to transition yet?"

The voice of my therapist, as always, gave me a connection to my future self that was a comfort to me as I felt myself beginning to fade from my life as Stephen. I was fully engaged in the leave-taking process and felt no fear or anxiety about it, and this I shared with my therapist.

I kept my eyes on the breaking dawn's light and felt a sort of rising sensation as if my body was pulling in two. Then the releasing feeling stopped, and I was aware of my breathing growing more shallow. I let the process happen as it would, without resistance. Odd how when one accepts, one is fine, I thought. Again came the release and return, although this time the release of the soul from the physical body seemed a longer interval.

I drifted on a tide of peace. Images flashed through my mind of myself as a young boy clambering up rocky hillsides and running after a herd of sheep in my father's meadow. The scene shifted, and I was that same young boy looking down at the dead faces of my parents as they lay in their crude wooden box coffins. I saw myself as a boy of twelve or fourteen approaching the door of the monastery—lost, alone, hungry, and grief-stricken.

It had been a good life, and now it was over.

With several heaving breaths, I released the soul that had inhabited the body I had known as Stephen and rushed forward into a light that shone with brilliance and joy.

"Marilou, now that you have released yourself from that life, it's time to return to the present."

Again came the tumbling sensation, as if I were being catapulted backward through a tunnel of alternating light and dark.

Soon I woke up on the couch, feeling very groggy and disoriented.

An intense drowsiness still engulfed me as I readapted to the time switch from distant past to present.

"Just relax for a bit. You've had a long journey, but it seems you learned a great many lessons during your life as the monk named Stephen."

I rested, and he continued. "I'm going to do some research on this lifetime of yours as a monk so that we have a way of measuring your lifetime progression. At our next session I should at least be able to share with you some more details of monastery life in Britain and where and when you may have lived as Stephen."

I stared at my therapist as he spoke, my eyes attempting to focus on his features. My body felt heavy and cumbersome. It took a while for me to come back, but I did so slowly and carefully.

The freedom of death and acceptance of it was still humming through me. It was as if an invisible umbilical cord still connected me to my life as Stephen. I knew I had to let it go and look upon that lifetime and the lessons that I had learned of humility, empathy, and kindness to my fellow humans.

I had found faith in God, very much enjoyed my work as a copier of manuscripts, felt comforted by the presence of others who were as lost and lonely as I was, found peace within despite my overwhelming urges to run away or sometimes voice my opinions. I had also developed a love of writing. The abbot had been much like the priest of my Atlantean days, and I had learned a great deal from him about temperament and compassion.

I had also again dealt with the issue of abandonment after my parents had died when I was young and then found love and acceptance in the company of those who were not of my blood but of my heart.

Later, when I left my therapist's office, I carried a portion of the peace of my life as Stephen with me into the turmoil of my present.

Thirteenth-century Wales

A few weeks before I went for this regression, I read an article about self-induced hypnosis, a method to access past-life memories on one's own. It seemed an easy enough thing to do and involved no ticking watches or focal points. It merely involved closing my eyes and relaxing to a deep degree, much as I did during sessions with my therapist and allowing whatever images arose in my mind to happen. There was a portion of instruction given, and one could either just memorize part of it or record it onto a tape player and play it back when ready to attempt a session. This article also directed one to have a notebook and pen ready after coming out of the session so that a drawing could be made of any outstanding mental images.

I decided to give it a try.

I didn't use any recording. I just pulled from the instructions the portions that I thought would help me to go solo back to a past life.

It was a cool and beautiful spring day when I settled back on a chair, closed my eyes, rested my hands on my lap, and allowed my thoughts to drift freely with no hindrance or instructions. As I did this, I felt the old, familiar pre-drowsiness come over me and let it happen. I then directed my thoughts and my soul self to take me to an important lifetime.

The first thing I felt was the sun shining hot on my head. Then came the voices of women chattering in a language at once foreign and yet familiar. The scene began to come into focus. I turned and looked behind me at a monstrous stone castle that crouched on the bank above me. I could smell mud and grass and hear water flowing swiftly over rocks, and I knew I was near a creek or stream.

And then the image abruptly ended, as if someone had hit the *Off* button on a television.

The screen of my mind was dark and silent.

Nothing more came, so I gradually brought myself back to awareness of the present and sat quietly for a few minutes looking out the window at the greening lawn, thinking perhaps that the aromas from outside had been what had tantalized my senses and given me the remarkable images.

But even if that were true, what about the castle? There were certainly none of those nearby, and I certainly did not have castles on my mind before the solo session. In fact, I hadn't thought about castles in many, many years. There were no voices outside my window that could have translated into the many women's voices talking in a foreign tongue. And there was no stream nearby.

No castle, stream, or voices.

Not one thing in my present moment could have been an inducement for what I saw in my mind.

But I could see that castle from my self-induced regression session so clearly. Every detail of the turrets, the high wall, the doorway below, and the stones it was made of all fitted together with great precision.

I picked up my pad and drew a very rough sketch of what I had seen. It wasn't much to look at, but I had done the best I could to remember the placement of each tower as well as the steep bank down to what I felt was a stream where I had been standing with the other women.

And that was it.

Years later I would receive a book from a friend in England. Going through it, I would turn the pages, and on one particular page stop and gasp in amazement, as I saw before me a photo of the castle that had been in my solo session and the edifice that would soon show up in my session with my therapist.

Validation came to me quite a while later, but it still came.

From the drawing I had made, the picture in the book, and my regressions, the place could be none other than Kidwelly Castle in Wales!

Before we began the session, my therapist shared with me a brief bit of the information he had found out about my monastery days. It seems that the Benedictine order was formed around 500 AD. I had been exactly right, he said, when I spoke as Stephen, that I was involved in all phases of work at the monastery and that I was unable to have contact with the outside world save for the people who came for help. I would not have been able to leave unless I had permission from the abbot.

I then shared with my therapist my findings after my self-hypnosis session.

Of course, he cautioned me against such things, but it was done and, at least to my mind, had garnered some good results.

This lifetime was not at all a surprise to me, as the Celtic and monk lifetimes were, and this was due in large part to my foreknowledge of some of it.

I was to find, however, that there had probably been a very good reason why my own self-hypnosis session had not given me all the details of this incarnation, because this session would reveal the tragedy of that life—a tragedy I should not have endured alone in my room at home.

As with my intense youthful fascination with all things Egyptian, there was also my attachment to the medieval times—most specifically, late-thirteenth-century Welsh history during the reign of King Edward the First, known as Long-shanks due to his physical build.

When I was a child I used to play at living in a castle. Oddly enough I often play-acted at being both a member of royalty and a laundress or a cook in one of the kitchens. This blend of social positions may have been a herald of the regression session I would undergo now during my adult life—and all of the elements, as well as quite a few more I had seen in my self-hypnosis session, would be present.

My therapist guided me in the usual manner.

I came into this lifetime almost as if I were simply picking up the threads of it and continuing with my daily routine. I knew I was a female and that I was somewhere between sixteen and eighteen years of age. I was standing by the bank of a good-sized stream and had apparently been washing laundry in the water. Above me the sun burned hot and uncomfortable. Insects buzzed incessantly around me. I wiped at my sweaty face with my cool, wet hands and found a momentary semblance of relief from the heat before bending again to my task.

I was not alone. Several other women of varying ages were also silently scrubbing and beating clothing on rocks and dipping them into the water, then laying the clothing on the bank to dry in the sun. There was only sporadic conversation and in a tongue quite foreign to me yet easily understandable. As I bent to my task I began to feel that I was somehow ostracized from the group.

When I stood up, my back ached horribly, and I reached around to rub at it.

That's when I noticed that I was pregnant and apparently in the later phase of the condition.

One of the women glanced over at me with contempt written on her face. She had reddish-brown hair and cold blue eyes. I almost shuddered from the scathing look she gave me, and I knew I would remember those eyes forever.

During this time I kept up my conversation with my therapist as I let him know what was happening.

Soon, we all in unison began to walk back up the hill. The journey was ponderous and took my breath away, yet I kept trudging upward. I didn't want any of the other women to know how difficult this was for me.

I don't remember re-entering the castle because quite suddenly the scene shifted, and I found myself alone in what would probably be termed a dungeon. The place smelled of manure, decay, and a fungal dampness.

I knew I was still in the castle. I was lying on a crude bed of old straw, and pains were racking my body in waves of agony. I did my best not to scream out.

There came to me the overwhelming knowledge that I was pregnant by a man stations above me and that we were not wed. The shamefulness of my situation washed over me as my body strained to release the infant within me that seemed determined not to be born this day.

Another image rose up in my mind of the babe's father. He was slim and brown-haired with the kindest sea-blue eyes and the nicest smile. He had shown me such kindness and compassion, and we had become friends and then lovers very quickly. Our love had been true and pure, but as he was above me in status we would never be allowed to wed, and yet despite this we had risked a physical relationship.

Now, because of my daring and my love and devotion to this beautiful man, I was about to face an excruciating death that would echo forward in time for many centuries and become a deeply soul-seated fear of childbirth.

Within my pain-racked body, agony seized and released me, alternating one to the other. I felt wetness seep from me, and the coppery tang of my own blood filled my nostrils.

I kept up a discourse with my therapist as I moved through the birthing process.

I reached down and felt for the child, and my hand came away coated with blood.

It came to me then that both I and the child were going to die this day, all alone, with no one to care about our passings.

"Ease into the death process, Marilou," came the distant sound of the therapist's voice. "If it is too painful, step away and observe from another angle."

I tried to pull myself away from the straining body on the bed of rancid straw but could not. The thing had a hold of me, and I knew it would not release me until my soul and the soul of the babe had flown.

The pains went on, and I found that I was falling into a deep sleep—a sleep from which I knew I would not awaken. There seemed to be a cottony-soft feel to the place I was moving through.

Physically, I felt a massive gush of blood leave my body, a release, and silence.

There was no other prelude to the event.

I tugged myself free of the now-dead self I had been.

My soul self drifted up above my horribly bloodied body and the dead body of my child and moved away and out through an open window cut high in the wall.

My last memory of that life was that of the women walking down to the river to again wash the clothing.

I drifted upward until the castle was no more than a toy-sized stone edifice far below me.

I never saw even a soul glimmer of the babe.

"Time to come back to the present, Marilou."

It was again very difficult to re-engage in my present body because this lifetime had taken a terrible toll on me.

A half-hour or so later, my therapist, who had been cajoling me to return to the present, acknowledged that with the reliving of my thirteenth-century Welsh lifetime I could now understand my intense fear of childbirth.

It is a fear, I believe, that will most likely follow me to all of my future lifetimes.

Native American

This was the only other time I attempted self-hypnosis before a session. As before I was at home, seated in my chair. I relaxed and closed my eyes, letting my mind drift along whatever pathways it would.

Within moments I seemed to be flying low, skimming across the ground above a summer's meadow. The sweet scent of the grass and the lushness of the field and surrounding forest enticed me. This experience was very reminiscent of my first dream visit with my grandparents after my grandfather died.

But this meadow didn't feel *heavenly*; it felt very real, and there were no waves of unconditional love flowing throughout—it was just a summer meadow.

I willed myself to come to a stop and drift down to Earth until I at last stood in the knee-high, breeze-blown grass.

Someone was coming.

Out the forest to my left a man appeared. He was slim with sleek black hair, and he had a bow slung on his shoulder and a pack with many arrows. He wore only a loincloth. I could not see his face, but I knew that he was an important part of my life.

The vision ended abruptly this time, as it had on the previous occasion with the medieval lifetime.

I waited but nothing more came to me, and I opened my eyes and sat contemplating the vision.

At the next session I would tell my therapist and again be cautioned about my inclination toward self-regression.

It would be the last time I would attempt to journey to a past life alone.

~

The regression session began as usual, and this time I seemed to glide seamlessly into the body I had inhabited in another time and place.

I looked around and found myself standing in the middle of a summer meadow. The tall, green grass was about knee-high and swished about occasionally as a gentle breeze moved through it. Above my head was a gorgeous blue sky with a few wispy clouds. The sun was warm, and the air was hot but not uncomfortably so. On all four sides of me there were tall trees of pine and fir, oak, and maple. To the far left, a small path meandered into the dense forest.

Just as I glanced down to see what I was dressed in, a piercing cry came from above me and I shaded my eyes to see what it might be.

A red-tailed hawk had flown out of the woods and was circling the meadow in smooth flight. I felt somehow that this bird of prey and I shared a connection but could not yet ascertain what that was. I watched the bird closely. It kept a watchful eye on the ground for any movement of life. I wished I could be like the bird and fly above the trees and into the sky so that I could see what lay beyond the area where I was standing. As these thoughts catapulted through me, a very deep yearning came over me.

I looked again at the forest path and realized that I was waiting for someone to come to me from that direction. Whoever it was had been gone for a long time, and I felt very alone and worried.

I kept up my communication with my therapist and told him about the path and my feelings about it.

While I waited, I took the opportunity to look down at my attire and found I was clad in some sort of dress made of soft animal hide. On my feet was a sort of shoe that looked like moccasins. I held up my arms and saw that they were a deep shade of reddish-brown. I then knew that I was a Native American woman and my age was about eighteen summers. When I wondered at my name, it was as if something whispered to me that it was Shadow Hawk. This realization was validation that I was spiritually linked to the hawk that had circled above me a few moments before but that had now left the meadow for better hunting grounds.

During this time I was keeping up a monotone dialogue with my therapist. He asked me if I could walk toward the little path and see if any memories might come back to me as to why I was alone on the meadow and who I might be waiting for.

For some reason I did not want to go toward that path but felt compelled to only because of my therapist's urging. I moved forward slowly and reluctantly. I sensed that it was a path that had taken someone from me whom I had deeply loved and might never see again.

I pushed through the tall grass and came to a halt at the point where the path entered the forest. The scents of pine and growing things filled my nostrils. I could see squirrels rushing up and down trees, and many birds flew away with beating wings when I approached their sanctuary.

I stood still and listened.

"Marilou. Are you at the path yet?"

I acknowledged that I was.

"Stand there and close your eyes and see if you can remember who it was that went down that path and has not yet returned."

I did not stand, but sat down on the meadow grass crosslegged and closed my eyes and waited for any sort of memory to come to me.

Suddenly, into my mind came the image of a tall, broadchested man who emanated an aura of strength and nobility. I somehow knew that he was of another tribe. He and I had been chosen for one another, yet despite this we had fallen deeply in love and had developed respect and understanding between us. We had only recently been joined together as mates in a ritual. A few days after the ceremony he had gone off on a hunting trip. In my mind's eye as Shadow Hawk I saw him walk toward the path, turn, and lift his hand, palm outward as if to wave farewell. The sun had crossed the sky for many days since he had left, and my heart was sinking in my chest because I had a premonition that he was no longer alive.

Doing my best not to show emotion, I stood and began to walk back across the meadow and through another forested area to my home.

There was a village that I belonged to, and it was situated near a stream. Many of the other women were harvesting and working in what appeared to be large garden plots. Children ran naked through the fields and splashed in the water—their shrieks of abandon now a bothersome thing to my heavily laden heart.

As I walked I imagined my mate lying dead on some distant forest trail, cut down in his prime by an unseen arrow. The image sickened me, yet I did not flinch from it but continued to move slowly along the worn dirt path to my home. This home was a sort of crude hut made of sticks laid together and tied by interlaced tree boughs. Mud had been pushed into the gaps in the tree limbs to keep out the cold. Several of the other members of my tribe passed by and looked at me with stony faces that registered sorrow for my situation. No words of condolence were spoken aloud, yet I sensed that they also felt that I was now alone in the world.

I wanted to grieve my loss but knew I could not. Any show of emotion was, I knew, seen as a sign of weakness.

I sensed that this lifetime was about strength and dealing with loss in a stoic and accepting manner.

The voice of my therapist intruded once again. "Marilou. I want you to move forward in time to the end of this life. When you get there, tell me what you see and if anyone is with you."

Again I felt as if I glided through my days until I found myself sitting in my stick abode. I knew it was winter. A fire burned in a pit in front of me, and I drew an animal skin that I thought was beaver around my chilled body. Several youngsters were seated around me in a circle, and they were watching me intently. I realized that I was very old. I pulled my braided hair forward and saw that it was white and felt very dry and brittle. My body beneath my dress felt withered, yet my mind was sharp and I sensed that during my later years that I had become a sort of sachem or holy person who imparted wisdom to the young through my stories and simple philosophies gleaned from the long life I had lived—a life I felt was well into my nineties.

The rapt eyes of the children wavered before me, and I next saw myself lying on a pallet of sweet-smelling pine boughs. I felt the agonizing feeling of trying to catch my breath and a pressure on my chest as if a large weight were pressing there. I could hear chanting around me and something like a rattle being shaken. It was still winter, and the winds howled outside as if trying to gain admittance and carry my soul away from the torment of being held fast in a body that no longer seemed to want me.

Before my eyes arose the face of my chosen one: he who had gone from my life so long ago never to return to me—until that moment.

He now stood in front of me as young and as vital as he had been when he had left me and traveled down that shaded forest path.

His dark eyes looked at me with a challenging compassion as he held out his arms to me. Exhilaration filled me with a last bit of strength.

With a final heaving breath, I reached out to him and it seemed he lifted me up and away from myself. I felt a sort of tugging sensation as if the body were reluctant to let go of my soul and then almost a pulling sound. I was free. I clung to my mate as we drifted above my physical body and looked down at it briefly. The chanting and the rattle sounds faded, and I slowly found I rejoiced in being unhindered by the lonely self I had been.

There are two side notes to this lifetime that bear mentioning. A few years after this session I met Dan, my present husband. In high school he'd had a great love of the game of lacrosse—a game that was, of course, played by the Iroquois Indians. Dan even physically resembled the man I had known was my chosen one in the Native American lifetime. The difference was the eyes—in that lifetime he had very dark eyes, and in this present lifetime he has blue eyes—yet there resided the same look of eagles as well as a piercing gaze. He has always had a great feeling of kinship to the Seneca tribe.

Then in the early 1990s Dan and I were visiting Gillette Castle State Park in Connecticut and eventually met a psychic there named Reverend Carl Hewitt. One day we were all standing on the pathway to the castle and talking. Suddenly, the psychic looked at me and told me that he knew I'd had a lifetime as a Native American and that I had been something like an elder or sachem of the tribe. He told me that many had come from near and far to listen to my words of wisdom and to be in my presence. I had been "very old" by the age standards of the day, and he saw me seated in a lodge and surrounded by many children and others who were listening to me with great intensity.

Dan was, as I said, with me when this occurred, and it was yet further validation to me that I had indeed lived that lifetime as Shadow Hawk and that I had been, for a time, revered by my tribe and by other tribes for my wisdom, insight, and storytelling ability.

Thus far my soul had lived in two ancient civilizations and the British Isles, and now I was on a new continent—North America. I sensed that my transition to this new world was for a very particular reason.

As I delved deeper into the people I had once been, I began to see a pattern of knowledge and wisdom being laid down in my soul mind, and I was anxious and excited to learn where the rest of the journey would lead me.

A Life in Salem, Massachusetts

This lifetime was about betrayal and learning forgiveness—the latter being a lesson I admit I still struggle with a bit to this day.

It was a little more difficult to descend into my life spent in Salem, Massachusetts, in the late 1600s, almost as if my soul knew the torment and treachery that awaited there. And let me preface this by saying that I have always had a deep-seated fear of anything to do with Salem and have never—despite the obvious allure of the place and many invites from family and friends to visit them there—even considered making the journey. Even though it lies only a few hours from my home, it is as if a force field of incredible soul-remembered agony keeps me at bay. To me and to most who deal in past-life regression therapy, this latent fear of a person, place, or thing is most definitely a sign of a lifetime connection that was not exactly joyful.

When I entered this past life it was winter. I knew I was a female and that my name began with the letter *M*, most likely Mary, and that I was somewhere in my twenties.

I was walking along a snow- and ice-crusted path, carrying a bundle of wood and a sack with bread in it. My face was numb from the cold, and my toes in a thin pair of shoes were so cold they felt as if they no longer were a part of my body.

Very few people were out that bitter winter's day, and the ones who did pass by seemed to intentionally ignore me. I could not discern why they treated me so, but as I trudged along, occasionally slipping on the ice, I began to feel as if I somehow deserved their disparaging glances.

Soon I came to a small cabin and went in. Upon entering, I felt a harsh and chilling rush of air from the single room, and that freezing blast actually felt colder than the outside I had just left behind. I tugged a woolen scarf from my head and placed the sack with the bread in it on a rough-hewn wooden table that was covered in dust. I walked across the mud-crusted wood floors to the grate, where long-burned-away wood ash lay white and gray. It was more than obvious that I had not been here in a long time. There was a deadness about the place that smelled of mustiness and disuse.

A deep sense of loss encompassed me, and I felt tears begin to prick at my eyes.

I put the meager supply of firewood on the floor, pulled up the sleeves of my dark woolen dress, and began to scrub at the grate with a handful of straw I found nearby. My first priority was to build a fire to warm the place. Once that was done, I could assess my surroundings.

I got filthy working on the grate but somehow finally managed to get the fire lit by hitting two pieces of what looked like stone together. It was slow-going and very frustrating, but at last a tiny spark caught on the bits of straw and twigs. My present-day self marveled at how I even knew how to perform this primitive fire-lighting ritual.

My therapist kept up a stream of questions interspersed with silence as I acclimated myself to this lifetime.

I stood and looked around the small, neglected one-room building. There was a table and two benches all laden with the filth of non-use. From where I stood with my back to the fireplace, I saw a sort of bed in the far right corner that had a raggedy quilt atop it. Of course the quilt was as filthy as the rest of the interior. There was a wooden bucket by the foot of the bed. I walked around the room, my numb feet in the thin shoes making no impression in the frozen and caked-on mud of the floors.

I moved to the side of the fireplace and made a startling discovery.

A small, handmade wooden cradle was there tucked into a corner as if abandoned.

I stared at it closely but could feel no attachment to it.

I went back to stand in front of the fireplace and held my chapped and aching hands out to catch even a modicum of warmth. While I stood there, I tried to remember anything at all about what may have happened to make this little place I knew was home feel so *empty*.

No thoughts came, so I decided to have a bit of bread as I felt very hungry.

The room was oh-so-slowly warming, but I could still see my breath in the air. I took a hunk of bread with me and stood by the fire.

Other feelings began assailing me as I stood eating.

Loss.

Regret.

Sorrow.

Anger.

And what I termed righteous indignation.

"What is happening, Marilou?" My therapist's voice again skittered through my swirling thoughts.

I told him that I was "pondering" what might have happened to me.

He responded that he would like to move me backward in time to the event that was of most importance.

Twirling, whirling, I rapidly moved into a vortex of the familiar alternating light and darkness until I became aware of cold, dampness, and the smell of earth and mud and decaying vegetation as well as a scent that was a bit more rancid.

I finally came to a stop and felt my body settle into this new scene.

It seemed that I had been dozing fitfully. Slowly I opened my eyes and looked around.

It was autumn, and I was crouched in a cage or small hut of the sort used for containing animals—perhaps pigs or goats. The ripe smell of manure now overlaid all the other scents and afflicted my nostrils. I looked down at myself and could see that a great deal of the foulness was on my clothing and that I stank of it.

My view was blocked by several homes and outbuildings. There were paths running off in different directions. I had been right—it was autumn and the scant amount of leaves that were left on the trees had turned to brilliant hues of red and golden.

Occasionally a citizen of the community would pass by the cage I was in and give me a disdainful look. Most ignored me.

I told my therapist where I was and what was happening.

Suddenly, a man in a dark outfit came up to the cage and bent down to undo a latch on the outside. He grabbed my arm roughly and hauled me out. I could barely stand because I had been crouching in that small prison for what I knew was a long time.

Painfully I felt my leg muscles loosen as I hobble-walked along beside him to another building. The man never spoke to me but pulled me forcefully forward. Several people stopped to watch me being treated so and whispered to one another. Their disdain for me was like the stinging-cold burn of ice lashing my soul.

My heart was weary, and I was shivering more with fear than from the damp chill that had settled into my bones.

I knew I had been betrayed by some of the same people who had once called themselves my friends.

I trudged along the icy path, my legs now tingling from the unaccustomed movement as I followed my jailer to a larger log building.

The man shoved me forward into a large, open room and pushed me to a rough-hewn bench near the front. I could see that several of the women I had known as friends were seated on another bench facing me, and they all had haughty looks on their faces and their demeanors were holier-than-thou.

I felt both shame and anger tear through me as I cast my eyes downward to the planks of the floor beneath my feet. I wanted so badly to rise up and go and scratch the eyes out of these women, but I stayed, quietly seething within.

A tall man stood up at a table and began talking. I knew he was somehow bringing charges against me for a crime I knew I hadn't committed, but his words were odd-sounding and garbled.

I began to fear for my life.

I folded my icy hands on my soiled dress and bowed my head.

There were many shouts of men's voices but I could not make out the words, only the anger and disgust of the tones. Some of the women were called upon to give testimony, and I began to know that I was being charged with adultery.

As near as I could make out, I was being tried for having had an affair with a man who had not been my spouse. I had no recollection of either a man in my life or an affair.

With my head still down, I leveled my eyes carefully and looked around the room but saw no one I recognized as a man I had loved.

There were more shouts. Several of the women pointed at me, their fingers accusing me—yet I knew in my heart that I was innocent and that the only crime here was jealousy of me.

Suddenly the door behind us opened, and a tall male figure entered. He walked past me and glanced down at me in pity; his striking blue eyes briefly smiled into mine, and the most overwhelming feeling came over me that this man was my savior.

He approached the man at the table and leaned in and whispered.

The room fell silent as everyone present strained to hear what was being said.

After a few moments that seemed to last much longer, the man behind the table gestured to me to come forward. I got up slowly and did as he instructed.

The kind man nodded at me reassuringly.

"You are free to go," the man said who had been sitting in judgment against me. "There has been a mistake. No charges are being brought against you. You have suffered enough from the loss of your babe and your husband."

There was no other explanation offered, and I didn't dare to ask any questions.

The news made me feel faint and I nearly toppled to the floor, but I regained my composure and made it to the door, not looking back.

I shall never forget the horribleness of betrayal I felt from ones who had called themselves my friends. It cut like a knife through my soul, and I knew that I would not easily be able to trust anyone—especially women—again. In fact, I felt I had been too trusting of others and determined to keep my own counsel and keep clear of any deep involvement with others.

My therapist urged me back to the cabin, and I was again standing in front of the weak fire. Around me the sense of loss hung in the air like a bitter frost. I had no real idea of what had transpired between the two men or why I had been so quickly released, other than being told I had suffered enough due to the loss of a child and my husband. I had no further knowledge of who my savior had been or what had happened to my husband. The only thing I remembered were the kindly and reassuring, oh-so-familiar blue eyes of the tall man who had saved me from what I truly believed had been certain death.

Returning to the present was tinged with a deep sadness. Betrayal tends to do that to a person—whether it happened centuries ago or in the present time.

This lifetime was yet another that would echo forward to my present day and create a gap with my attempts to trust others with my deepest self. I had learned to keep my own counsel, to remain quiet and to observe. I constantly questioned the motives of others who wanted to get close to me, and I did not trust most people. I developed an uncanny sixth sense about human nature and recoiled from any situation that felt false. It seemed that almost every time I did attempt to have a close relationship with women, I found again some of the same problems I had experienced in Salem—and this was very sad because I yearned for a true friend who would be like a sister to me. Someone I could share my deepest feelings and dreams with—but each attempt failed. Maybe it was because I expected the betrayal and thus created a sort of self-fulfilling prophecy.

Maybe I just picked the wrong women to befriend.

In any event, when the relationship failed I did forgive these women and attempt to move forward.

Yet I could never forget the pain they inflicted on my psyche with their leave-takings.

Each lifetime was now—at least to my mind—plainly seen as a building block, one atop the other as I moved forward into my future selves.

The Victorian Era

Cameos, lace, tea parties, long dresses that swished silken or velvety, horse-drawn carriage rides—a time of family and togetherness and harmony.

I fell in love with the whole time span from the 1850s onward when I was about six and reading the Sherlock Holmes detective stories. At that time I also had several favorite authors: Mark Twain, Charles Dickens, Edgar Allan Poe, Louisa May Alcott, and Harriet Beecher Stowe.

I, of course, had no idea that at least two of these authors would echo into my future life as a writer and bring me back in touch with that engrossingly charming period in history.

It would also reunite me with a young man I would fall in love with whom I knew I had loved and lost during the American Civil War—he being the one in my dream as a sixteen-year-old in my present lifetime.

Further, I'd had in my twenties yet another vocation I wished to pursue—that of being a part of the stage as either an actress or a playwright. Circumstances would rise up to prevent me from being able to embrace that most desired choice of heading to or returning to Broadway—as I again somehow knew that I had once walked the boards of many theaters in various cities across America and Europe.

I was now noticing that my lifetimes thus far seemed to come centuries apart, yet when I descended into my lifetime in the mid-1860s, I felt somehow rested and renewed and ready for my journey. I did not have any difficulty in descending into my past self.

I had a knowing that I was female, in my mid-twenties, single, an actress, and that my name was Amelia. I lived in New York State and had come from a very loving and well-off family. I believe I had an older sister and that she and I were close, although I felt she was married and out of the home.

I found myself in a beautifully appointed parlor room suited out with plush maroon velvet sofas and chairs. There was a fireplace, the mantel of which was a residence for many photos in small frames. The ambience of the room was lovely, and the areas that I could see beyond where I sat working on a piece of needlework were also notable for being quite well done. I could see into the next room, where a large dining table with a lace cloth atop it brought images of wonderful meals and good family times. The corner of a glass-fronted china closet was also visible. A sound from the window across the way made me look up, and as I watched, a golden-furred cat leapt down and stretched and walked past me, brushing its body against my skirt as it headed to the dining room.

Outside the window I could see flower gardens full of an array of glorious blossoms and green-leafed trees. A breeze caused one of these limbs to sway and gently tap the side of the house.

The ambience was one of gentility, peacefulness, and a knowing that I had somehow contributed through my own efforts to this marvelous life of ease.

The sound of a door closing came as a soft thud from somewhere in a room to my left. I put my needlework in a basket next to the chair and got up and followed the noise. I found myself in a kitchen area, where a heavyset woman with graying blond hair was busy taking some carrots and other vegetables out of a wooden basket and laying them on a table.

She looked up at me, curtsied quickly. "Good afternoon, miss. Dinner will be ready soon. Would you like tea or lemonade?"

I acknowledged that I was fine and thanked her. When I returned to the parlor, my eyes landed on a photograph on a side table. This photo was of a very handsome young man in a blue uniform. He was blond-haired and his eyes looked dark, but I knew they were the most beautiful blue. I had a rush of deep emotions overtake me for this handsome man, feelings that blended into deep romantic love, fear, and longing. I knew also that he was deeply important to me but could not totally ascertain if the feelings were of a romantic nature or protective, such as one would have for a dearly loved and missed brother, cousin, or neighbor.

This was a puzzlement.

I had the oddest commingling of emotions course through me as I stood silently and gazed at that face.

I knew that his name was Nathan.

Who was he to me to cause such overwhelming feelings?

The voice of my therapist cut through my senses, tugging relentlessly at me when all I really wanted to do was to ponder this sweet man's face.

"Marilou! Where are you? What are you doing?"

I responded quickly with the details of what I was experiencing and broke off my ponderings when there was a knock at the front door.

The maid answered, and a tall, distinguished man with brown hair and deep-set blue eyes doffed his hat and asked for me.

I did not recognize this man at once, but it came to me that he was William and he had something to do with my career on the stage.

Again, the voice of my therapist came to me.

"Who is there with you? What is happening?"

I told him who I was with.

There was a ring of near-frustration in his voice.

He wanted me to move forward in time.

Even though I was very curious about William, it was very difficult to resist the urge to stay in the present moment.

The next scene found me on a stage, pacing back and forth and holding several pages of a play in my hand. I was apparently learning my lines and movements. The tall man, William, was seated in the front row offstage and was prompting me to move differently, lower my voice, and create a mood.

I did as he instructed, and a few minutes later he yelled out, "Bravo!" and began to applaud. This made me feel absolutely wonderful, and I curtsied in response.

Another woman, slim and blond, came onto the stage and began speaking her lines. For some reason I did not like this woman at all, and it was apparent she felt the same about me.

I never got to see myself in the part I had been rehearsing, as my therapist moved me further ahead to my past as Amelia. Quick, sharp images came to me. I was in a house by a river with a woman I knew was my sister, and it was nearing twilight. A sound of horse hoofbeats outside. I ran out of the front door heedless of the fact that it was early winter and that I only had thin slippers on my feet.

It wasn't long before the wet on the grass quickly soaked through the slippers, turning my toes icy cold, but I didn't care. A young man in a dark blue uniform rode up and handed me a rolled-up paper. This man was very handsome, tall and lean, with chin-length brown hair and steady brown eyes. I had the sense that he was a spy during the Civil War and that he may have been a relative. The man looked down at me fondly from his chestnut-colored horse and then rode off up a field and along a dirt path by the river.

I went back inside with the papers and never knew what happened after that. Many years later I would re-meet this young man at an office where I was employed as a secretary. Again, I recognized him because of his eyes, but his build, his hair, and his demeanor were all exactly the same as they had been in the 1860s. When we met, or re-met, we fell instantly into easy conversation in that now-familiar seamless fashion that happens when souls reunite across time. It was if we were simply catching up. Once I tested him by asking him what he thought about the Civil War. Without hesitation, he replied, "It was total waste!"

The voice of my therapist again tugged at me. "Marilou! Let's go and find the young man in the photo! When you get there, tell me if you are with him or someone else."

I felt as if I were yanked from the scene with the young man and pulled backward into the now-familiar alternating light and darkness. I found myself standing on a country road. To my left were fields of dried, late-autumn grass. To my right a shallow river moved around a bend and disappeared. I felt that this was the same river from the previous vision. A young man—the one in the photo I had looked at in the parlor—was with me. He was dressed in the blue uniform of a Union soldier. He stood in front of me, holding the reins of a large gray horse. When he leaned down to kiss me, I fairly leapt into his strong arms and returned the kiss that was both tender and forceful as I put every bit of my emotions into it.

I sensed he was saying goodbye—and somehow I knew it could be for a very long time, possibly forever.

I also sensed that he and I were not married but betrothed.

I watched with tears falling from my eyes and a lump in my throat that I could not speak past as he mounted his horse and rode off slowly, looking back only once to wave. And then as if he could no longer bear the leave-taking, he kicked the horse into a gallop and rode off down and around the bend and was gone from my vision.

My therapist now urged me to go ahead in time to my death as Amelia.

I found myself at an age between thirty and forty. I had no idea what had brought me to my deathbed, but I sensed a great tiredness that seemed to have settled into the very marrow of my bones. I was lying on a sofa in a parlor, but it didn't seem like the previous home I had been in. I did not know what season of the year it was, nor did I care. There were people whispering all around me but I could see no forms or faces. And I paid no real attention to them as I became more fully involved in the transitioning process. During these moments my heart would speed up and then seem to diminish so greatly in acceleration that it was a barely imperceptible organ in my chest. Anxiety and peace warred within me as I struggled to both stay and leave this world behind.

I seemed to be floating in a timeless void where I began to wish the whole process could just be over with so that I could be free.

Suddenly before my mind's eye came the vision of my betrothed. He was standing in his uniform with arms outstretched. I began to mentally tug and almost forcibly try to free myself from my physical body so that I could get to him before he vanished. At last I felt my soul give way, and there was an intense feeling of release and relief as I rushed forward into his arms.

When I came back to the present a short time after this transition experience, I found, to my surprise, that I was not weary but refreshed. The experience had left a feeling of deep peace behind in my present body, and I actually yawned and stretched in contentment.

Every one of my sessions had taught me several things.

Life is indeed eternal.

Death is freedom and release.

Love is forever.

A DETECTIVE

It would seem that my future plans for career choices were many and varied, and based on positions I had enjoyed in other distant times and places. From my very earliest days I knew I wanted to be a writer and to help people. Then as I began to attend elementary school, I wanted to be an archeologist and uncover the treasures of ancient Egypt. Even though I was not directly involved in them, the Salem witch trials both fascinated and repelled me, and in my early thirties I actually considered the idea of becoming involved in Wicca but just as quickly discarded the thought. But casting back to my youth, by the time I was almost nine I was becoming fascinated with the world of detectives. Of course my favorite detective was Sherlock Holmes. Grandpa began buying me books about Holmes. He also bought me the *Classics Illustrated* comic books about Holmes's exploits, and I read them cover to cover in one day. I still have these treasured books in my bookcase today.

By the time I was in my early teens I had somehow dropped the idea of being an archeologist, and I yearned to fight crime and bring bad guys to justice. I wanted to find a way to bypass being a patrol officer and go straight to detective work—but, sadly, when I was in school in the 1950s and 1960s, that sort of thing wasn't really offered in the college curriculum as a career choice for women. Choices were pretty much limited to girls growing up to be wives, mothers, nurses, teachers, or secretaries. There wasn't much calling, at least in my high school, to announce to my guidance counselor that I wanted to be a forensic detective—and I don't recall the path of becoming a detective ever being offered or discussed. My guidance counselor, dear person that he was, told me that it would be best if I applied my innate talent for typing and shorthand into a college course that would serve me for life—secretarial training.

I never thought to balk.

By the time I was in my late twenties and early thirties and before I had ever experienced a regression session, I had strange visions that would come to me out of the blue. I had a very clear image of myself as a male detective being shot in the back and at a restaurant. For some reason I had an abhorrence of seeing lines at a restaurant, especially where people were waiting and leaning against a wall. I always felt claustrophobic and trapped when I was in such a situation. I feared for the people who were standing there innocently, and this fear was most unreasonable as I had no precedent for any anxiety about lines in my present life. In fact, I recalled that this fear went all the way back to my kindergarten and elementary school days when we children were lined up to go to the cafeteria. It seems that only eating establishments bothered me. Still, this deep-seated fear was a clear linkage from the *knowing* that I had been a male detective in a large city.

My musical tastes also echoed the 1920s and 1930s, when the big bands were in abundance and gangsters like Al Capone ruled the underworld of crime. In my thirties I even purchased a book that taught the foxtrot and learned—or relearned—how to do this dance. The smooth sound of a clarinet blended with a tinkling of piano keys—and maybe a violin, horn, and drumbeat—would set my senses afire with longing for something, a time that seemed to me just out of reach. In later years I purchased many LPs and cassette tapes of the music of the era—all the while not really knowing why I was so drawn to it.

As time moved forward, other things began to manifest in my life—things that seemed to serve as guideposts to the past and the present coming together.

⌒

When I arrived for my session and was made comfortable, my regression began promptly. I was surprised at how quickly I descended into this lifetime. I found myself walking briskly along a damp sidewalk. It was late at night and streetlights were on. A few people moved past me, and I hugged the wall near the shop windows I passed. I knew it was winter as evidenced by the chill air, but I was not sure which month. It felt like December or maybe early January.

Oddly enough, I was able to quickly catch a glimpse of myself as I paused by one of the shop windows. I appeared to be a male, slim and of good height. I had brown or dark hair, a fairly nice-looking face, and kind yet wary eyes. I looked to be of Italian descent, or maybe Welsh or Irish. I had a sense that my name may have been John or started with the letter *J*.

I sensed that I was single, about thirty years old, and that I was a detective—and it was a job I deeply cared about.

The city felt gritty, like either New York or Chicago, and it was the late 1920s or early 1930s.

Furthermore, my life, like the city I was in, also had a gritty feel to it, as if emotions and feelings inside me had been wrenched out of place on a soul level.

I had a sense that despite my youthfulness and apparent charming good looks, I had been hardened by the things I had seen of human nature. I had witnessed man's inhumanity to man on a pretty grand scale. There had been interactions with the mob, an incredible amount of bloodshed of both the guilty and the innocent in the names of both justice and revenge.

I wondered as I walked along that sidewalk which one, or more, of the people I was passing had connections to the crime families in the city. Who was recently released from jail or prison? Who might be out this night to commit a horrible deed against others?

I knew how quickly a simple day could turn into one of horror, and I kept every one of my senses on full alert as though I was waiting for the proverbial next shoe to fall. I even checked to make sure my off-duty revolver was with me.

My stomach rumbled, and I was alerted to the fact that I hadn't eaten much since breakfast. Up ahead was a restaurant. I paused. It suddenly came to me that I was supposed to meet someone at this place.

A woman.

I had a date!

That was why I was hurrying.

I seemed to move with a purpose through the area and kept my eyes peeled for any nefarious activity. There was about that day a heightened sense of urgency, as if every step I took brought me closer to something bad yet destined. Even though I was keen on my surroundings, I could see nothing out of the ordinary around me.

I went into the restaurant, up some stairs, and saw my date at a table. She was a small-framed, dark-haired woman —very pretty and very nice. An orchestra was playing some dance music.

I don't remember eating—I only remember dancing with the woman in my arms. I could feel her soft hair brushing against my chin, and feel my arm around her and her hand in mine. We glided easily together to the music. An intense jolt of genuine love for this woman hit me as I held her, and I was so grateful to have found her. As we danced I also knew I had conflicting feelings about marrying her because of my job. I felt that I was engaged to her or that there had been talk of marrying.

Then, like one of those old-fashioned black-and-white TV screens from my youth, the picture of our dancing seemed to roll and stop halfway down. Brief snatches of memory came. The dance floor beneath my feet. The way I seemed to fit into my body with ease—a smell of spicy food and cigarette smoke and the woman talking to me in words I could not make out. Voices all around me, flooding my senses, nearly building to a crescendo and then fading until there was only the woman and me and nothing more seemed to matter.

I started to relax.

This was a mistake.

Everything from the time I was dancing onward was a blur. I remember running, my heart pumping in fear and anger. I remember people screaming and crying and an overwhelming feeling of destiny.

There were frantic people lining up by a wall. The robbers had instructed them to do so, and they also ordered me to do the same.

I fired my revolver at a man and he fired back.

Incredible pain lanced through my body.

I knew I'd been shot and in the back.

I couldn't breathe.

Blackness began to descend quickly to try to claim me.

My brain was dazed, as if some part of me were standing off to the side of my body and could not comprehend that this had happened to me.

I fought the darkness while I felt life fading from my damaged body.

My most intense fear—the one that froze me—was, oddly, not the fact that I was dying but that I couldn't seem to get my legs to move anymore. In fact, I couldn't feel them or any part of me.

I could hear my therapist's voice yelling at me from an incredibly great distance. Breathlessly, I tried to tell him what was happening. He gave me the now-familiar movie screen admonition as I approached transition from my physical body. It was almost too late, and I found I did not have the strength to follow his directions.

I seemed to be totally numb and slipping away from myself and rapidly becoming detached from my physical body.

I didn't want the encroaching darkness to claim me and I tried to fight it off, but its force was gaining strength while I grew weaker and less attached to my body by the second.

I did not know if any life-saving techniques were given to me.

I really didn't care.

I let go of life with great reluctance and sadness—sadness for all the things I knew I would never have the chance to experience.

Sadness for the loved ones I was leaving behind who I knew would not recover from losing me—their lives forever altered and tainted by my sudden absence.

This lifetime I had almost grabbed that brass ring and experienced it all: a loving family, a job I took great pride in, and, at last, love with a woman who seemed my equal.

All of it gone in the space of a heartbeat.

I could hear my therapist's voice coming to me as if from a very great distance, but I didn't pay any heed to it. He, of course, was very anxious because I had moved so quickly into my physical death without any real assistance.

Voices faded into the distance. I lost all sensation of being alive. I left with so many regrets for the life I knew I had lost.

Coming out of this regression was almost more difficult than when I had returned from my medieval lifetime.

The dazed and bewildered feelings stayed with me for many days, and I couldn't seem to shake the morbidness of that lifetime.

I felt drained and helpless and so very sad.

On the way home I pondered the thing over and over.

I had done my duty but lost my life.

Had I been brave or foolish?

Too late now.

I also had another memory rise up in my mind that I believe was a premonition of this past life.

It was winter and I was probably about nine or ten. My grandparents and I had just gotten out of church. I was in the backseat of the car. As we drove past the church, I happened to glance over at it with the morning sun striking the front, and instantly a great fear clenched at my heart, which began pounding furiously. Into my mind came the shouted words: "You died in your thirties and your funeral was at a Catholic church!"

This fearsome thought that came out of nowhere very nearly catapulted me into an asthma attack, so swiftly and harshly did the message come. There had been no warning, no precursors to it happening—it just lashed out at me and was shocking and horrible for me to comprehend.

With no comprehension of a past life when I had died in my thirties, I lived in fear that the message had meant I was to die in this lifetime in my thirties. I well remember when I reached my fortieth birthday that I breathed a sigh of relief. Of course by then I had put two and two together and realized that perhaps that shouted mental message had something to do with this past lifetime of being a detective.

But I had learned a valuable lesson from this lifetime as a detective that would resonate into my present day: life is precious—don't squander your time here, because it can all be over in an instant.

During the next few weeks the memories of that horrendous session faded somewhat.

Over the years intervening from then to now, I would see an ad for a college degree in forensics working with a police department. My greatest wish was to be able to open cold-case files and utilize the mindset I'd had as a detective in another time—but again, how could I dare to say to a college administrator or a police chief that I knew I could do the job because

I'd been a cop and a detective in another lifetime? It would hardly work out. So, I soothed my longing by watching some of those detective reality shows on television—but it wasn't the same. The calling was still there, seeming to tug at me from a distance, but as the years passed and I got older, I knew that those dreams of being a detective were far behind me. Who knows? Maybe I was being protected by some larger force that was keeping me away from that line of work because it had had such a tragic effect on my previous life.

The years passed, and except for brief cringes when I had to wait in a line at a restaurant, the detective lifetime faded from my mind. Oh, there were incidents that happened that pricked at my mind and gave me a vague feeling of connection to that lifetime. One of those incidents occurred every time I heard Barry Manilow sing "Copacabana." Even before my regression to the detective lifetime, this song tore at my heart for no apparent reason. Fast forward a few years, and I finally understood—the story of a night-club death was my story in another time and place.

As if to rise up and remind me of the tragedy of my lifetime as a detective, a dream came to me a few years ago, and I shared the dream with Dan.

This dream took place at a local restaurant. It was winter, and Dan and I had been seated and were getting ready to order. I had a very uneasy feeling and kept glancing over at the doorway. Anxiety welled up inside me, and I tried to keep it at bay. I had the overwhelming urge to get out of the place quickly or hide under the table.

Suddenly, in through the doorway burst a group of men with weapons. Two women were on either side of the men. The *killers*—because that is the word that resonated in my brain—tried to get everyone to stand and line up. I ducked beneath a table. Dan was nowhere to be seen. I heard shots and screams of terror and agony. Then all was eerily silent.

I heard moans and crying and stayed put.

I don't remember coming out from under the table. I don't remember anything after that except waking up shaking and anxiety-ridden with my heart pounding furiously in my chest.

After calming a bit with a hot cup of chamomile tea, I chastised myself for being a coward in that dream scenario. Even though I knew I had no weapon, I felt inadequate and somehow responsible for the carnage that my dream eyes never looked upon.

Weeks later I pondered briefly my detective lifetime and wondered if the dream had somehow coincided with the date of my death in that last lifetime. The season had been the same, but the time of the dream was in the present day and since I had no date of my death as the detective, I could not be certain. Still, it was another point to think about. What if on certain days of our present life we are feeling ill or out of sorts because on that day in one of our past lives we died or were dying?

Could the echoes of those past-life death days echo into our future lives?

It was an interesting thing to think about.

After this last session, I no longer went to see my therapist. He was in the middle of making a career decision to move away to a place where his interest in past-life regression could be better utilized. I was in the midst of the divorce process and concerned about the future of my niece and nephew.

I did try to find my therapist in the mid-1990s, at about the same time I attempted to find my mentor from the office, but to no avail.

Then, just days after I finished writing this book, in December of 2012, I decided to give one last try at finding my office mentor. The search was made easier because I now owned a computer, something I had not had in the '90s. As with everything in life, the timing was perfect, and we connected on the phone, less than an hour after I searched for her.

We spent an amazing hour or so catching up on the years apart—which numbered about twenty-seven. We laughed and reminisced about the day she reawakened me to my past lives and put my feet on the spiritual path I was meant to follow—but she wanted to make two things clear to me: first, that she be allowed to remain anonymous; and, second, that it really wasn't she who brought me such enlightenment. Rather, it was God and the guardians of my own soul that spoke through her and gave me the lessons I needed during the time we spent together in the 1980s. This information from spirit came, she said, from "my higher self."

I also had the marvelous opportunity of being able to thank her for all she had done for me. She is now in her early seventies, and her voice is still calm and soothing, her wisdom intact, and her kindness still shines and resonates in every word she spoke to me. It is truly a blessing to have reunited with her again in this lifetime, and we both plan on not losing touch again.

Update on the Detective Lifetime

Miracles happen every day, and one came into my life a little over two years ago when I found, quite by chance, information on a police officer/detective whose tragic end seemed to closely parallel my past-life memory. I am not stating that this man is who I was, but there are many similarities. Now, through the grace of the universe and probably many other higher beings, I am in the process of writing the biography of this incredibly brave man, and I am so very honored to be doing so.

Looking Back

I have to admit that during the time I was being regressed to my past lives, there was a part of me that stood off to the side and wondered if I were somehow making up the whole thing. The experience of being regressed sometimes—well, most of the time—seemed surreal, at least to me.

Then, I thought, if I were making it up, why would I have chosen some of the lifetimes I did? I mean, the Egyptian incarnation is okay as it was a lifetime of wealth and power. But why a lowly monk, why nearly a human sacrifice, why a woman who died a horrible death in childbirth, a woman scorned and betrayed by friends and community, or a Native American who lived out a lonely existence when her mate died? Wouldn't it have been better to imagine myself as a queen or at least a person of power, fame, and wealth in all of my incarnations?

Seems reasonable.

And that realization—that clarity of understanding of the diversity, the trauma, the sadness commingled with moments of peace—is what brought home to me that none of this was my imagination. It was far too *real*. And that included the sensations of the regression sessions. When I was taken back in time, I was totally and fully involved in the place. I could smell the sea breezes, feel the wind on my face, feel the warmth of the sun. In the Atlantean lifetime I felt the excitement and joy of being able to levitate, and when I descended to the stone steps I felt the coldness of that stone on the backs of my thighs and through my gauzy robe.

Every one of my senses was heightened by my experiences.

In the therapist's office there were no scents, sounds, or textures that could have served to create the things I was feeling.

And so, I surmised that it had been real. I had lived as those people in those other times. Their souls and mine were one and the same. We were all one forever and ever, and the connection would never be broken because we had been born and lived and loved and laughed and cried and then died and returned again to earthly life. The story is neverending. The soul—my soul—has spent eons learning and growing and yearning for *home*, and that is the miracle and the hope and the joy of knowing and believing and being thankful for every lifetime lived.

And it follows that when the curtain of doubt about the reality of reincarnation is stripped away, there is an incredible change inside. How can one then fear death—or life? There is continuation and reunion and learning that is ongoing, and I, speaking for myself, know that my life—or lives to come—will never be the same.

HERE AND NOW

All of my previous lifetimes have now culminated into this one. I still carry the skills, the talents, the fears, the hopes, and the dreams in my soul that I had back in those distant times. I love learning, fear betrayal, have a near-obsessive urge to keep my laundry done, love to write, love to research history (my answer to not being able to be a detective this time around), and remain interested in the Civil War and the theater.

Most people wonder if in a past life they were a queen or king, a princess, or someone very wealthy or powerful. If the proof is in the knowing, only one of my past lives had anything to do with wealth and that was the Egyptian lifetime— but it apparently didn't matter to me, as I willingly left that lifetime behind because someone I loved was not to be found.

And the same could be somewhat said of the Victorian life. I still died relatively young and without the love that I so desperately craved.

So much for wealth and position.

All I know is this: I am so grateful that this present-day life has brought me into contact with those I have loved and learned from in another time—and this includes those who have brought me the hardest lessons of all.

Chapter Five

THE RELATIONSHIPS

During our all-too-brief time together, Butch and I had no words for what we were feeling, but, as at our first meeting, there was an overwhelming sense of *familiarity*, as if we had done this all before in some other place or time. When we touched, it was very nearly electric; and when we kissed tenderly or held hands, there was a feeling for me of being transported to peace and an eternal joy that obliterated all but us. His touch provided a link of strength that transcended anything I had ever encountered up to that point. It was so very much more than just two young people in love: it was as if our flesh was one and the same—as if the same heart and mind that were within him were also within me. This cosmic link eventually would become even more of an eternal bond when Butch passed to spirit in 1990 at the age of thirty-eight, and came to me in a dream just moments after he died to tell me of his passing.

Butch and I always expressed to one another how amazing it was that we felt so incredibly comfortable with one another from the day of that first meeting. Again, neither of us had words for what we were feeling, but we both constantly admitted to one another that it was "like we were meeting again after a long time apart" or had "come home." There was also a deep *knowing* that often swept through me that he was, like me, *old* on a great many levels. I never really felt that Butch was ever a teenager, but rather that when he was fifteen he was more like eighty because of the knowledge he had of human nature. He was a sage who gave advice that only someone very ancient could give—and he did it all with kindness and compassion and a tenderness that belied his youthful earth age.

Often when he was occupied with something like watching TV, or when I was seated next to him in his car, I would gaze at him intently. Perhaps he was aware of my scrutiny, perhaps not. But when I did do this to him there seemed, at times, to be a sort of glow around him that had nothing to do with the external light of the sun or any lamps on in a room. This would appear to be almost like another presence that hovered just around his physical body—and then, when I would blink my eyes or look away from him and back again, the glow was gone. I often thought I imagined it—years later I would come to know that I had not.

But one day stands out in my mind with remarkable clarity, almost as if there were a mental photograph taken by me to have so that I could recall the moment for the future.

Butch and I were on our way to his home, which was about an hour or so distant from mine. It was the summer of 1968, and the day was gorgeous. The sun was shining but was not overly hot. Butch already had the top down on his

Plymouth Fury convertible. He had come to meet me at his aunt and uncle's house just down the road from my home. We left quickly that day, anxious to be on the road and alone so we could revel in the joy of just being young and escaping the prying eyes of the grown-ups who were trying their best to keep our growing affection for one another under control.

As usual I was seated next to Butch, our legs pressed together, the radio on, the feeling of freedom zinging through our souls. Just as we were about to pull out onto the highway, I looked at Butch closely. His brown, wavy hair was reflecting a golden glow; his face in side profile seemed somehow frozen in time. He turned and winked at me as he felt my gaze on him, smiled that heartbreakingly beautiful off-sided grin that always melted my heart, and made me feel warm and loved and protected.

There were no words between us—just peace.

The image was captured in my mind's eye as significant for some reason, but I let it go, as Butch reached over, took my hand in his, interlaced his fingers through mine, and rested our clasped-together hands atop his thigh. I rested my head on his shoulder as he pulled out onto the highway.

I drifted along and don't really remember the roads we took or the time passing—external things drifted far away from us, and we were enveloped in a sort of snug and loving cocoon of perfect happiness because that was the flavor of the days we spent together.

It wasn't until I had my regression sessions a little over fifteen years later that I at last recognized Butch as the young boy who had been with me in the Atlantean temple—and I did that not only because of his oh-so-familiar eyes, but also because his profile from those ancient times and his frozen-in-time profile in that car during the summer of 1968 had been exactly the same.

One other telling thing with Butch was another game he and I often played when we were apart. Late at night, when everyone in our respective homes was in bed and both houses quiet, we would play the "Sending Game"—that is, at about ten or so at night, we would both be in our rooms and would attempt to link telepathically and send a mental image to one another across the sixty-five or so miles that separated us. When we wrote to one another or during our treasured fifteen-minute biweekly phone calls, we would share what we had telepathically transmitted to one another. With only a small amount of deviation, we were usually right on! Of course, again with no pre-knowledge of any past lives spent together, we were exactly re-enacting the game the priest had us play in Atlantis!

Sadly, despite Butch and I having such a close and marvelous reunion in this lifetime, the relationship ended when I went off to college in 1969. We had been together for a little over three years. In recent years some of his friends shared with me that he had been told to write a break-up letter to me. This may or may not be true.

In my heart I have always believed that Butch left because he had taught me all he could during this lifetime, and that was the reason things ended between us.

And in the end it really doesn't matter how or why—it matters that it did end, at least for us to be physically together.

He had a choice to make as a young man, and he did what he thought was right at the time.

As those who have read my book *Dreaming of the Dead: Personal Stories of Comfort and Hope* know, Butch has been with me in spirit ever since his passing in 1990, and we are once again able to share a remarkable love that is still eternal and full of joy and the hope of reunion once more.

The dream of the Akashic Records, the regressions, and my own childhood memories all combined to bring into my life those with whom I had karmic debt or those with whom I had shared love, kindness, and friendship.

Indeed, again it was brought home to me that we meet exactly who we are supposed to meet when we are supposed to meet them and that we have been reborn at precisely the right time to come together once more.

Of course, my relationship with my Civil War soldier echoes forward in time also—not only to my premonition dream of him when I was age sixteen, but also of an event that occurred while I was visiting a museum in Vermont when I was in my twenties.

I had wandered into one of the rooms, and there was a staircase. On the wall was an enormous oil painting of a man with chin-length blond hair and astonishing blue eyes, wearing the uniform of a Union soldier. I was riveted to this painting and took a picture of it.

Something about the eyes drew me in and seemed to say, *This is important to you. Remember it in the future!*

Almost as if an invisible clock were ticking, the man and I did meet not too many years after this Vermont visit. He and I would marry and spend about six years together before divorcing. I have always thought that all we needed was a completion of the lifetime when he rode off along the river trail and never returned—until his soul came back in a body remarkably similar to the one he'd had over a hundred and twenty years in the past.

Then I re-met Dan, who had been my beloved in my Native American lifetime, and as of 2014, we have been together for twenty-six years. Oddly enough and speaking of echoes from past lives, I still get very anxious and nearly cry whenever he leaves me to go any distance. This resonates to that lifetime when he went off down the forest path and never returned.

And then there is my Atlantean priest, who instructed me in so many things when I was his student. Who was he in this lifetime? Did his dear soul return to help me along my path?

I believe he did—and that he was none other than British actor Jeremy Brett, who came into my life in the 1980s via television one night when Dan and I were switching through the channels to find a show to watch. It was the eyes that were so very familiar and so full of wisdom that caused the now-accustomed zing to course through me.

A short while after this, I was in both letter and phone communication with Jeremy, and he once more became my mentor—the man who constantly urged me to follow my dreams of being a writer, who urged me to "never give up," and who, when he passed to spirit, came to tell me of the event and then returned to me in dream visits on several other occasions.

He will forever remain a blessing to me, and I miss his physical presence every day.

But he remains with me every day in spirit and is never far away when I need his sage advice.

I would like to say that every one of my re-meetings in this lifetime was full of love and compassion and kindness. But that is not so. Like all humans who have trod the world, and still do, just encased in different bodies—there have to be some negative meetings.

When I was young and met someone for the first time, I either instantly liked or disliked the person.

Some innate sixth sense somehow took over, and even as an infant I could feel a *darkness* swirling around some people who came into my days. I could not talk, of course, with words, but I remember making my feelings known by screaming at the top of my lungs whenever one of these undesirables came near me. I was only comforted by the presence of my grandparents, and never really developed that acceptance or tolerance of those adults who liked to chuck me under the chin or speak to me in baby talk. This was an abomination to me, especially as I retained my memory of conversations dealing with philosophical topics and advanced mental capabilities. In all of my lifetimes, despite my youthfulness I had been treated as an adult and a valued member of the society in which I found myself.

Sometimes, even now, people will ask me, "Have you ever met someone that you instantly disliked? Someone you didn't even know existed until that moment but that you can't wait to get away from?"

I have to admit I have.

Then there is the flip side of that: "Have you ever met someone for the first time and felt so comfortable with them that you end up talking for hours as if you are catching up on old times?"

I joyfully admit that I have.

I cannot, with any degree of authority, state that all meetings with people in the present have anything to do with past lives—sometimes I think that the person we are meeting has qualities of a good or bad experience we had in another time or place. Unless some of the feelings of attachment or repulsion are present, someone is exactly what they appear to be: a newly met person. For example, as a young child I never liked women with red hair who wore dark-framed glasses. I had no idea why I had this intense dislike, but in later years found that one of my aunts had been such a woman. I don't know if my infant self had perhaps sensed her disinterest or disregard for me as a person—but whatever it was, red hair and dark-framed glasses were fused in my mind as things to avoid.

Again, I don't believe that every single relationship we have with another person or even an animal is a past-life one. But there are definite telling signs that there is a shared connection from another time, and those are, of course, the intense attraction or repulsion about some physical or character trait evidenced in that being.

Oddly, many of my present-day, negative past-life relationship meet-ups have happened at work sites. This spot has always seemed to me the perfect place for real lessons to be learned. What better forum for learning to forgive and release than working in close proximity with someone who, perhaps in a past life, was your mortal enemy—or you were theirs? In a workplace there must be teamwork and everyone has to maintain a level of professionalism, so that a common goal of productivity can be reached. Throw in someone that you have to work with who was a thorn in your side in another life, and you have the makings for some serious lessons to be learned on both sides.

If, as I came to believe, relationships define us for good or ill, then perhaps there is a new way to look at them—especially the negative ones.

Chapter Six

A PRESENT-DAY
LIFETIME READING

Once again destiny intervenes, this time in the form of a wonderful woman named Elizabeth Crowley. I have never had the privilege of meeting Elizabeth in person in this lifetime, but we did link up after she wrote a great review of my book *Dreaming of the Dead* on Amazon.com. As I have found to be typical when two souls are meant to meet or connect again, the timing of the event was pure perfection. And I must make note that Elizabeth stated in her review of my book that she felt "compelled" to get in touch with me and that this was something she had not done with other authors whose works she had reviewed.

So it came about in May of 2013 that Elizabeth contacted me because she was wondering if she could do a distant individual reading for me. I suggested a past-life reading that could be included in this book. We both knew we were onto something, and so we began.

I have to admit this was a lot different from the sit-down regression sessions I had with my therapist in the 1980s. But much like the aftermath of those sessions, I experienced several bouts of extreme weariness that found me taking many unexpected naps as the drain on my soul self happened. I have always been very sensitive to anything to do with a reading of my higher self, and so this weariness was not unexpected. I deeply felt the tug and pull of someone digging around in my aura, and my body seems to compensate by putting my physical form to sleep so that I can be somewhat rejuvenated.

It should be stated at the outset that Elizabeth was aware of my relationship with Butch in this lifetime after reviewing my previous book. She also asked me which of my past-life connections I would like to know more about, and of course I said Butch. And again, I did not tell her anything of the other lifetimes I had shared with Butch, so in essence this reading is incredible because, as we shall find out later, it resonates with the truth of a career change and choice Butch had made just prior to his death in 1990.

Elizabeth tuned in to a lifetime I lived in Canterbury, England. I feel that this lifetime was just prior to my Victorian one when I was an actress. During the lifetime I lived in Canterbury, Elizabeth heard from her spirit guide, Master Guide Eric, that my name was Julia. I am also given a different aspect of my life there with the boy I knew as Butch in this present incarnation, and when I view the tapestry of our lives together, it all makes sense that we reunited in 1967.

Here is the rest of the reading Elizabeth did for me:

"There was an illness in your family. Master Guide Eric stated that your father was ill, but then your entire family fell ill. You received consolation from your spiritual mentor, who was Butch. He was your teacher. There was something really unusual about him. He was more like a New Age healer. He talked to you about perception. He also tried to heal you. He also administered medication to you. However, I also hear him recommending some prayers to you. I hear him saying, 'These two prayers will help.'

"You felt you owed this person very much. To Julia, he was a very competent man. But others saw him differently. I did not hear his name. But in this incarnation Butch was very charming. I heard he was one of a kind. He was close to Julia's ideal. There was a strong attraction from the beginning. But both of you thought it would have been unnatural for there to be anything more—at least at first. Although Julia spent a lot of time with this man, it seemed more spiritual than religious. No one questioned it at first. No one even questioned that a young lady would be spending time with this man. Master Guide Eric said that everyone was very mindful, but this eventually changed when it grew into a romance. People started to warn Julia's family that she was spending too much time alone with this person.

"Although this was not the intention, a love relationship did eventually develop, but it was very dysfunctional. He was a very jealous and possessive man. I hear someone saying, 'I don't want to get caught.' There was also talk of birth control. I heard a conversation about birth control, but it was explained in a way like birth control was still not quite understood or readily available.

"So, this person was Julia's spiritual teacher, and both of you helped others to awaken to their spiritual path. Eric said that you both were great awakeners. Julia was also very clairaudient in this incarnation. She was also a medium. Julia even had hopes of writing. Your desire to write comes partly from this incarnation. But it seems Julia's writing was more of a way of expressing herself and speaking her mind.

"Julia would eventually leave Canterbury, England, with her mentor and they would get married. But it is not apparent whether they married before or after they left England in search of a cure for the family's illness. Julia was apparently apprehensive about this journey. Not only would it be a long one, but she was also worried that she would not speak the language. It was not clear where she went, but she did end up in a place where there were many wild animals that she wished the royal family could see. Julia also went on this journey to be an apprentice to her husband. During that time there was a great deal of multitasking. This may have been during a war or time of upheaval…Julia experienced moments of great joy during this trip.

"Julia and her husband had a daughter in this incarnation. Master Guide Eric stated that her name was Libby. However, after the birth of the child, Julia's perception of her husband changed. There were some aspects of her husband that she did not like. I also hear that Julia's husband did not know how to love. There were arguments. I heard someone screaming, 'I'm not trying to escape you!' I also hear the other scream, 'Liar!' It looks like the end of Julia's life was very lonely. She may have lived somewhere deserted. She died in her home, possibly with her daughter, Libby. Eric said that Julia welcomed death.

So, she was definitely tired of a life where she was no longer happy with her husband. Although there was a strong romantic and intellectual attraction in the beginning, the birth of the child changed everything for the worse."

Elizabeth went on to state that during my lifetime as Julia, I developed problems with trusting others but that I kept this to myself. My husband in that lifetime and I, despite the ups and downs in the relationship, did go on to help many people spiritually. One of the life lessons I had as Julia was to learn to deal with challenges and turn them into something positive, which I did accomplish.

Butch and I went through a great many challenges in that lifetime, as Elizabeth noted all great romances do—but apparently we cared enough for one another to reunite once more.

There is such an incredible amount of this reading that rings true for me—most of it having to do with the medical aspect of my present life. Butch was always very interested in my angelic healing from asthma just prior to our meeting, and he remarked on how "special" I was to have had such an experience. As my life experiences had taught me up to that point in time when we reconnected, I felt both blessed and at the same time nonchalant about healings. I now know I shouldn't have, but at sixteen, I did. At that age, finally free of the dis-ease that had made my life a misery and falling in love with the most gorgeous and compassionate of boys— well, the world seemed golden.

It was just recently that I found out from someone who knew Butch very, very well that he had wanted to give up all the perks of his life and job in New York City to become a pediatrician and that he had actually been accepted at a university to begin his studies there.

Butch, who had been a healer in another time—who had given me perception of my own life and who had consoled and loved me—did spiritually heal me and many others during his brief sojourn here in this lifetime. His greatest gift of healing children may not have been realized, but he left behind a legacy for me of more than that—he left me with his eternal love.

Chapter Seven

ON THE PATH

I have always felt that I was most fortunate to have been born, or reborn, into the time period that has spanned from the early 1950s to the present day. I grew up during a time of innocence. The Great Depression was behind us; Eisenhower was president; and, several years later, songs like "Aquarius/Let the Sunshine In" by the 5th Dimension were lighting up the airways and spinning as vinyl on my record player. This song—indeed all the songs—as well as the era of love, standing up for what one believed in even though it wasn't a popular idea, expanding ways of thinking: it all became part of my psyche, and I believe gave me the courage to write and to speak aloud about what I had experienced since I was a young child.

But the timing had to be right.

Even though as a teenager I had no idea of what my past lives had been, I was still a product of those long-ago times. I had learned humility, empathy, and sympathy. I had been honed by the fires of betrayal and jealousy, and when I saw injustice in this present lifetime I lost all fear of retaliation, because I lived by the motto Butch and I had moved through our days with—the one about not doing anything to anyone else that you wouldn't want done to you. And, indeed, it was Butch who was one of the first ones in my life who encouraged me to let go and let my heart and feelings rule my deeds—to always seek balance between firmness and gentleness, to confront uncomfortable topics that had too long been kept in the shadows and to bring them into the light of day where meaningful conversation about them could take place.

It was with Butch's urging that I confronted an uncomfortable topic in high school—a silent monster that roamed the hallways of my school.

I recall that we seniors all had to give a final speech for our speech class. Most of the kids in my graduating class of 1969 chose relatively safe topics. I looked around one day while I was getting my textbooks out of my locker and had a major epiphany. There was great disparity among the students in my high school. There were those whose last names were of note in the community because their dads were doctors, professors, teachers, lawyers, and so forth. Mainly due to this caste system, most of those students seemed to be able to live by different rules than the rest of us. There were the "haves" and the "have nots," and I could plainly see that a mentality was operating that shoved people like me aside. I never yearned for popularity or glory on the sports field, but I also did not think it fair that many of us were looked down upon or barely noticed.

The school hierarchy seemed set in stone. And each one of these groups seemed to be divided into cliques—students who basically stuck to their own kind and never dared or even wanted, in my estimation, to cross the line in between and care about us "have nots."

Maybe I was right in what I was feeling and seeing around me—maybe I was wrong—but within my youthful self, anger was taking hold because what I was seeing around me was unfair. At that time, of course, I had no knowledge of my past life in Salem, but something must have echoed forward in time to my teenage self from those days. Perhaps it was the shunning, the non-acknowledgement—but whatever it was, it hurt me deeply and I wanted to do something about it to bring about some sort of awakening among my classmates.

Even though I was concerned with being ridiculed or ignored, I just knew that it couldn't get any worse—and that gave me courage.

I mulled the idea over with Butch, and he told me, "Go for it!"

So it was that a few days after my locker epiphany, I decided to try an experiment. Coming out of English and on my way to my next class, I dared to say hello to a cheerleader in the hallway. She turned her head and looked at me in surprise and then hurried past me as if I didn't exist.

I knew then that I had the topic for my final speech and the means to get off my chest the feelings of hurt that had cascaded through me at that cheerleader's rebuff.

My speech, "Cliques in High School," garnered me a good grade, the admiration of my English teacher and her student teacher, and oddly enough it somewhat erased the demarcation lines between me and *them*. In fact, the next day, many of the cheerleaders and a few others who had shunned me for years began to say hello to me in the hallways. A small victory to be sure, but it was a start. That speech also set the stage for my growing sense of fearlessness about speaking my mind, even when the subject matter might not be popular with family, friends, or my community.

As a side note: that speech is still remembered and spoken of today, well over forty years later, by certain of my classmates that I meet or talk to on the phone or via the Internet.

Just as the speech about cliques took the same type of courage I had exhibited during my Celtic lifetime when I had taken charge and dared to alter the course of a near-tragic event for the good, daring to speak out about what I perceived as wrong opened doorways hitherto closed. Likewise, speaking or writing about the subjects of ghosts and reincarnation takes courage, but that courage emits a sort of radar of fearlessness to those with open minds.

Yes, it takes courage and faith to speak out to the world about such topics, and I honor every single person who writes about these subjects or goes out and speaks openly about them to the world at large.

And people do seem to be waking up.

At a great many of the speaking engagements I give throughout the year, the conversation somehow slides away from the spirit realm and my near-death experiences to the subject of reincarnation.

And that is so wonderful to me.

This topic—like ghosts and the afterlife—is no longer being kept in the shadows and whispered about. It is all out in the open, and as I stated at the beginning of this book, there is among the people I have met an awakening and a restless dissatisfaction with the old ways of thinking.

And this is a remarkable and wonderful thing.

On the gravestone of actor William Powell's wife Diana "Mousie" (Lewis) Powell, in Desert Memorial Park in Cathedral City, California, is the inscription "We'll Meet Again."

To me, that simple three-word sentence says it all.

Diana was the third wife of William Powell, who is best known for his portrayal of Nick Charles in *The Thin Man* series of movies with actress Myrna Loy. Diana and William were married for forty-four contented and peaceful years, and from all reports—and despite an age difference—they were united at a soul level with a definite eternal connection that could very well find them returning to be together in some other time.

And there are many, many others who, like Diana, have been famous and believed in reincarnation. Today, the likes of Willie Nelson and Martin Sheen are believers in reincarnation. Ringo Starr, Dennis Weaver, George Harrison, and of course the Dalai Lama are or were also believers, as were other names from history such as Benjamin Franklin, Henry Ford, and General George S. Patton—and the list goes on.

All of these people were, for the most part, profoundly affected by their past lives.

Yes, I truly believe that we will all meet again in other times and places, if there is a need to complete what we never got to finish with one another—be it for good or not so good. Love, especially, creates a bond that I know death cannot destroy, because it has happened in my own life.

My first love, Butch, who is ever-present with me in spirit, was once more nearby when I recently lost a local playwright contest. As Dan and I were waiting in the lobby of the theater to get the results, his essence and the aroma most connected with him—the scent of clothing freshly dried on the line and spray starch—swirled around me. The next, most amazing thing was the sound of our very favorite song, "Incense and Peppermints" by the Strawberry Alarm Clock, coming from the stage area, where it was obviously a part of the performance that day.

Again, as I do not believe in coincidence but I do believe in timing, and realizing that if I had been a moment later I would not have heard this beloved song, I knew Butch was nearby, seemingly trying to get my attention. He knew that I had not won, and as he always had done in life, he was very concerned about my feelings being hurt and was most likely warning me away.

I know in my heart that Butch and I will meet again—if not in another lifetime, at least in the afterlife. And perhaps if we are granted another lifetime together, we will either pick up the threads of our youthful love or maybe we will return and work together in a profession that helps people— either way, it is a very comforting thought, because between us I know that the story isn't over.

Most certainly Dan and I will share a portion of our next lives together, because we have, like Butch and I, forged a bond that is eternal.

I must also remark that my mother's deep-seated belief that we were once sisters is most likely an echo from my Egyptian lifetime. I have often had quick flashes of memory of walking with her through an ancient marketplace, and we were either twins or very close in age.

After all is said and done, there is no scientific proof that rebirth or reincarnation is real, but like so many who have trod this path before, I know in my heart that our souls return, reborn in new bodies to complete our journeys forward, to right the wrongs we have done to others, to learn and grow and love again, before returning to our eternal home forever.

AFTERWORD

And so I found that I had lived a total of ten prior lifetimes, and the present one makes eleven. As fantastic as my story may sound, I can only tell it from my heart and exactly as it happened and is still happening to me.

I did have a reawakening to the memory of my past lives at the age of three months as I lay in my grandmother's arms. I had the dreams of the future and the distant past at age sixteen, as well as being healed of pneumonia and asthma by the compassionate touch of my guardian angel. I have had three near-death experiences, and during the last one I was taken to Heaven by my guardian angel, where I briefly reunited with my loved ones and pets that had passed to spirit through both form and dream visits from them.

It has been an absolutely incredible journey to be here on Earth once more and to have a new body and a new life. I have reunited with my beloved ones across centuries of time, renewed old friendships, and known the joy of looking into the eyes of a dear one and feeling that zing of recognition. I have also met with those who were my enemies in other times and places, and instead of returning betrayal, jealousy, and hatred to them when they have attempted to resurrect the old hurts, I have given them forgiveness, love, and peace, and thus forever broken the karmic debts that have been between us.

It is all miraculous, and the story is still ongoing and very exciting.

When I was young—and that is up until the time of my regression sessions—I lived in what I term a one-dimensional world. Life went on seamlessly and was bordered by a routine and a mindset that had been laid down for me by the dictates of family, friends, and society. It was, I must admit, a comfortable time, and it would have been so very easy to have stayed there, following the path that never deviated from the cradle to the grave. Home, church, work, marriage, children, retirement, and death.

Even though that path works for many, it did not resonate for me. As a female this lifetime, I was expected to play my part in the limited world I inhabited: to be a "good girl" and then die a good death. If I stayed within the confines of how I "should" act and react to life, I would be labeled as "good" by my family, neighbors, and community at large. If I deviated from that path and dared to think outside the box and question the status quo, I would be shunned—and quickly.

When my soul began to awaken to other possibilities about my life on Earth this time around, its true meaning and direction, I admit I did falter. I was torn between the "right" way and the new way of thinking. I hesitated, but only briefly.

It began with talking with my mentor at the office—no, it actually began with my talking to Butch about my feelings, my dreams, my fears, and all the rest. It began with him encouraging me to give that speech in high school and his praise and pride in me when I became courageous enough to speak out about what I saw as wrong and hurtful. Because, as I've said, it does take courage to wrench away from the tried and familiar and to at least be willing to question and wonder about different topics like reincarnation.

I never, ever thought that I would one day step back from the beliefs my dear grandparents had instilled in me and strike out on my own path. But I did, and by doing so I have lost some old friends and found new ones with minds that are open to acceptance and who are not afraid to wonder and ask that question, "*What if?*"

Anyone who has knowledge of their past lives knows that each lifetime builds one upon the other. Each of my lifetimes has been filled with all the range of emotions allowed we humans: joy, sorrow, loss, reunion, betrayal, love, jealousy, greed, and remorse. I have found and lost people who meant a great deal to me both then and now. I have been born into wealth and power and abject poverty of mind, body, and spirit. I have transgressed because of love and paid for it with my life. I have been on top of the world as well as in the depths of despair.

But none of it has been in vain.

All the lessons accumulated over the centuries have been experiences my soul has needed to complete a cycle of learning so that eventually my soul can return for good to that place called *home*—a journey I believe we are all on.

Looking back from this vantage point, I feel that I have lived miraculous lives. I have been a student in one of the most magnificent civilizations that ever existed and have wandered through Atlantean temples of pure beauty. I have had remarkable teachers who truly cared about my advancement on the path of life. During my lifetime in ancient Egypt, I meandered sedately through sunlit temples as a young girl. In that incarnation I had the most wonderful family.

Finding my lifetime in the British Isles as a monk who secretly wrote poetry, and both yearned for and feared the freedom that lay outside my window, was beautiful because it is so like me in the present-day incarnation. Dying as a lowly laundress in Wales while giving birth to my beloved's child taught me great humility and also that love, all love, has a price that can echo forward in time. Even the bad experiences I had in the Celtic or Salem lifetimes only served to prepare me for the future. The Native American lifetime saw me losing the man I loved yet also living to a ripe old age in a place where I was revered for my wisdom and compassion. The detective lifetime taught me again the lesson of humility and about thinking before I act. It also taught me to take nothing for granted.

Reincarnation has never been proven as fact, yet there is so much evidence provided by pioneers in the field: Dr. Ian Stevenson for one and also Dr. Brian Weiss, who stumbled upon a past life quite by accident while he was working with a patient riddled with anxiety. Totally skeptical at first, Dr. Weiss became a believer when the woman began to channel information from the spirit realm and messages from his dead son.

And there are those like myself who know beyond knowing that they have lived before and that many of the prior lifetimes span the centuries. To me, it is absolutely incredible that I lived during the times of the past that came through in my sessions. I could never have imagined them, and if I had, I believe I would not have chosen a few of the lifetimes—especially the ones filled with pain and loss and tragedy. I probably would have imagined better lives filled with love and wealth and joy, as many of us would.

Over the centuries that my soul has inhabited different bodies and lived in varied places, I have learned both empathy and sympathy for my fellow human travelers. I have also learned to forgive others as well as myself and move on. Acceptance has been key for me, and although it has not been easy, I have done the best I can with the circumstances I have found myself involved in and have learned these most valuable lessons:

Make the most of the time you spend here on Earth.

Harm no one.

Be kind to all life forms, and also be kind to yourself.

Keep an open mind.
Realize that love is eternal.

I wish you the very best on your journey.

THE END—or a new beginning?

And then I awoke and found I had been
Born again.
I was a baby once more with a new body and a new life.
And somewhere out there you were a baby as well
Or soon would be
And soon our story would begin again.
—Marilou Trask-Curtin

To Write to the Author

If you wish to contact the author or would like more information about this book, please write to the author in care of Llewellyn Worldwide Ltd. and we will forward your request. Both the author and publisher appreciate hearing from you and learning of your enjoyment of this book and how it has helped you. Llewellyn Worldwide Ltd. cannot guarantee that every letter written to the author can be answered, but all will be forwarded. Please write to:

Marilou Trask-Curtin
⁒ Llewellyn Worldwide
2143 Wooddale Drive
Woodbury, MN 55125-2989

Please enclose a self-addressed stamped envelope for reply, or $1.00 to cover costs. If outside the USA, enclose an international postal reply coupon.

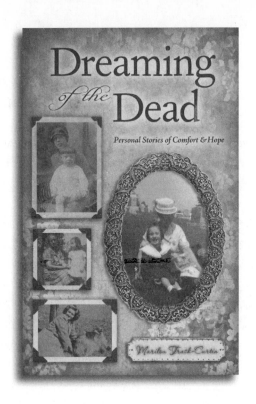

Dreaming *of the* Dead

Personal Stories of Comfort & Hope

Marilou Trask-Curtin

Dreaming of the Dead
Personal Stories of Comfort and Hope
MARILOU TRASK-CURTIN

Ever since a near-death experience when she was very young, Marilou Trask-Curtin has been able to communicate with spirits, primarily in unusually vivid and realistic dreams. Over the years she has seen many spirits and has communicated with her first love, her beloved grandfather, and even British actor Jeremy Brett, with whom she'd grown close through years of correspondence. The spirits come to offer advice, reassurance, or to let her know they have died or are about to—this includes her companion animals, who return to show they're as full of health and joy as their human counterparts in spirit. The author also tells of dream visits from historical "mentor" figures such as Samuel L. Clemens and Harriet Beecher Stowe, as well as many others. *Dreaming of the Dead* offers readers an incredibly compelling journey to the world that awaits us all on the other side of life's doorway.

978-0-7387-3191-9, 240 pp., 6 x 9   **$15.95**

MEMORIES
of the
AFTERLIFE

Life Between Lives
Stories of Personal Transformation

Edited by
MICHAEL
NEWTON, PH.D.

with case studies by members of the
NEWTON INSTITUTE

Memories of the Afterlife
Life Between Lives Stories of Personal Transformation
MICHAEL NEWTON

Dr. Michael Newton, bestselling author of *Journey of Souls* and *Destiny of Souls*, returns as the editor and analyst of a series of amazing case studies that highlight the profound impact of spiritual regression on people's everyday lives.

These fascinating true accounts are handpicked and presented by Life Between Lives hypnotherapists certified by the Newton Institute. They feature case studies of real people embarking on life-changing spiritual journeys after recalling their memories of the afterlife: reuniting with soul mates and personal spirit guides, and discovering the ramifications of life and body choices, love relationships, and dreams by communing with their immortal souls. As gems of self-knowledge are revealed, dramatic epiphanies result, enabling these ordinary people to understand adversity in their lives, find emotional healing, realize their true purpose, and forever enrich their lives with new meaning.

978-0-7387-1527-8, 336 pp., 6 x 9　　　　　　　**$17.95**

miraculous moments

True Stories Affirming that Life Goes On

ELISSA AL-CHOKHACHY

Miraculous Moments
True Stories Affirming that Life Goes On
Elissa Al-Chokhachy

Does life go on after death? Will we ever be reunited with loved ones? Does love ever die?

Heartfelt testimony to the everlasting human spirit can be found in this wondrous collection of true stories from people who've seen, heard, and felt love from beyond. Laugh along with the husband who enjoys one last April Fools' joke from his deceased wife. Rejoice with the family who are reassured by the presence of their father and husband, whose life was lost on September 11, 2001.

Told with courage and warmth, these vivid accounts—hugs from family members who've passed, sightings of souls leaving a body at the time of death, encounters with angels, near-death experiences, and even visits from the spirits of beloved pets—offer hope, reassurance, and comfort to anyone who is mourning a lost loved one or has ever wondered about life after death.

978-0-7387-2122-4, 312 pp., 6 x 9   **$17.95**

Past Lives

For Beginners

A Guide to Reincarnation & Techniques
to Improve Your Present Life

DOUGLAS DE LONG